Ramblings of an Outdated Old Coot

JEREMY GORMAN

Ramblings of an Outdated Old Coot

BETTERING TOMORROW WITH PAST INSIGHTS

2009

Ramblings of an Outdated Old Coot

CONTENTS

INTRODUCTION

No one can be around as long as I have and not see major changes in society. Many of these changes are good—some are not. Somehow, we take for granted those that are good, but complain bitterly about those we don't like. "Ramblings" takes another point of view—if you don't have a better way, keep quiet. It is easy to find fault, but hard to find a solution.

Note that I said <u>a</u> solution. I am not presumptuous enough to assume that my solution is the best one. It is <u>a</u> solution. The purpose of this book is to get people thinking about how to solve the inevitable problems that arise in a diverse world. Together we may come up with <u>the</u> solution. If Ramblings can stimulate even a few of those solutions, I will be delighted—and hopefully you will too.

The thing that sets man apart from other life forms is his ability to cooperate. Together we can do wonders. This book is about involvement—<u>your</u> involvement. When we can do so much in cooperation, why do we spend so much of our time fighting? Cooperation lifts all boats. Fighting sinks them.

So here it is. I invite you to enjoy Ramblings. You may agree or disagree, but remember, don't bitch—find a better way!

Jeremy Gorman

RAMBLINGS

CHAPTER 1
Universal Health Care—A Pipe Dream?

The cost of health care has been rising at twice the rate of inflation for about 30 years. It continues to rise at almost 14%/yr. and may be getting worse. The health care industry is very creative and devises marvelous new treatments and procedures. But the health care industry is a business. It needs to make money. The net result is that it develops myriad new treatments. However, the industry does not produce many cures or preventions. All the new high-tech drugs and procedures are long term. Many of the vaccines we have today were developed 30 or 40 years ago, because there is no money in prevention. If Pfizer developed a drug that cured arthritis, it would be used once—not daily for thirty years. So Pfizer has many arthritis drugs and has become one of the most profitable companies in the country. The cost of treating arthritis continues to rise as they develop ever better and more extensive treatments.

It is worth studying why healthcare has seen such radical increases. There is no doubt that the technology has improved dramatically. We treat things we didn't even know about in 1950. Drugs are available for every ailment you can imagine. Just look at your television screen, and find that about one quarter of the ads are for some pill or elixir or machine that will treat your medical symptoms. "Sure, go ahead and eat burgers and fries every day and gain sixty pounds—we have a marvelous pill and a diet plan to fix it." But none of those pills actually cures the problem! At best they manage it. Treating symptoms is a long-range project, and a bonanza for drug manufacturers.

There is a better way. We spend billions of dollars each year developing new drugs, new procedures and new machines to treat the ills of society. From headaches to Alzheimer's disease there is a pill or procedure to relieve the symptoms or control the progress of the disease. Those dollars have created a medical marvel. There is hardly an ailment we can't treat. But the focus remains on treatment—not prevention or cure. That approach has created an overwhelming increase in medical costs.

Doctors, drug manufacturers and medical instrument companies are making money on treatment. Prevention would reduce their income—not increase it. There is no incentive to prevent disease if your business is treating it! And it's even worse if you manage it long term. Yet our government spends literally billions of your tax dollars supporting development of these "miracle drugs". 44% of medical research in the U.S. is supported by government subsidy. Taxpayers spent $28.4 billion on drug research in 2005.

Very few medicines prevent or cure the diseases or conditions. If you take an arthritis drug, for example, you'll take it for the rest of your life. Some of the antibiotics do cure infections, and are used up in a week or so. But most are long-term programs. Almost none of them <u>prevents</u> a disease. We do have a few vaccines that actually prevent measles, polio, flu or pneumonia. But if you were at Pfizer, which would you prefer to make, Measles Vaccine, or Viagra?

Developing a universal health care system will be an impossible task if costs continue to grow at such high rates. How can we put the brakes on such inflating health care costs? One way is to look at the current system and see why it is out of control. The Department of Health and Human Services (HHS) and its subsidiaries the Food and Drug Administration (FDA) and the National Institute of Health (NIH) subsidize the drug companies to the tune of $4.9 billion a year. This goes to one of the most profitable industries on earth—19.7% last year. Grants to the drug industry are desirable, but should be much better controlled. For example: No research grant should be made to any drug company for development of treatments—only for prevention or cure. The results of research are rarely accurately predictable. If a drug company develops a treatment with their research instead of a cure, that's OK, but they should be taxed 20% of their profits until the grant is repaid twofold or threefold. Drug companies are perfectly capable of supporting their own research on profitable treatments. Since they are remarkably profitable that is where their research efforts go. But American drug companies that accept those federal grants then charge the American citizen that supplied the grant more than any other country for the drugs that they develop. That is immoral and ought to be illegal. It is outrageous that American made drugs can be purchased for less in any other country other than our own. Your tax dollars should not be fed into that process. So, in addition to repaying the grant, there should be a ceiling on the profit margins of drugs developed by companies that accept federal grant money.

It is much harder to get the attention of a healthy person on medical procedures than the guy who has just entered the emergency room. Television ads feature treatment—not cure. Of course! It is in the best interest of the advertiser. The drug and instrument manufacturers will make huge profits on many new drugs and instruments they devise to treat many ailments that are self-imposed. Obesity is getting to be a serious national problem. Although it is largely a result if the prepared food industry that makes delicious, but unhealthy food ubiquitous, it is at least in part due to the many drugs and treatments that lower cholesterol, reduce high blood pressure or clear out plaques from the blood vessels. They literally invite you to eat bad things because they can then cure you. But obesity is largely self-imposed. Why should tax dollars pay to develop profitable treatments for avoidable ailments? Tax dollars should support prevention and education rather than control. Teach people how to eat a healthy diet rather than treat the problems after they occur. Plenty of us will require management and control to keep the treatment industry thriving. But it would be better if fewer of us needed it.

Another way to achieve affordable universal health care is to do it stepwise. We should first pass a law that supplies prevention or cure for every citizen. Not for treatment, or sustaining—just for preventions or cures that already exist. It is peculiar how practices change to follow sources of money. When prevention and cure dollars are assured, more effort will be applied to prevention and cure. This will have a measurable effect on health care costs. As we gain control of health care costs, the law might be expanded to cover certain treatments whose numbers will expand as the costs become manageable.

Drugs are not the only source of waste in our medical system. We have a more complex issue of diagnostic tests. Currently the more tests you run on a patient, the more Medicaid, Medicare and other medical insurance plans pay. That is aggravated by the litigious nature of our society, in which we sue others for anything that happens to us. This is largely because lawyers entice patients to sue for large settlements so that they can receive a 25%, 33% or even a 50% fee. Doctors, whose malpractice insurance premiums have skyrocketed, will run as many tests as possible to avoid being sued for negligence, which will further increase their already exorbitant premiums. Since insurance pays for the tests, run as many as you can and avoid being sued. We need a law that restricts lawyer's fees to 15% on medical malpractice suits. That would slow down the lawsuit explosion, and allow doctors to run tests as they see fit, instead of what some hot-shot lawyer thinks is fit. Let's have a medical system, not a legal one. In that system, we should require hospitals and clinics to show good cause for running expensive diagnostic tests of doubtful pertinence to the case at hand. Today, when a patient shows symptoms, doctors and hospitals run batteries of tests to analyze them in minute detail. But relatively few ailments require all that testing. Many years ago my doctor found my heart problem in his office with a stethoscope. He ordered a battery of tests. The diagnosis didn't change at all, but it cost me $5000.

I suggest that government oversight committees, in cooperation with hospitals and physicians, (not insurance companies) establish a series of test procedures for various symptoms. If the first level identifies the problem, no more tests are run. If not the second level of tests is ordered. If that identifies the problem no more tests are run. If not, the third and fourth stages are ordered as needed.

Perhaps we should also consider an excess profits tax for industries that dominate any public services. We had them in WWII, and they did prevent some excessive gouging of Uncle Sam by military subcontractors. When a company gains dominance of a vital resource, it should then be held accountable for its equitable delivery. Such anti-monopoly (antitrust) laws have existed for a long time. They were used to break up Standard Oil before 1920, and to break up AT&T. If profit is the sole reason for making a drug, perhaps we should consider another drug.

Most industrialized nations have national health care programs. Our American one is operated by insurance companies, and provides less coverage to a smaller percentage of people and for a greater cost. It strongly supports those who have enough resources to afford health care as opposed to those who don't. We hear loud and dire warnings from them about having a nationally operated or universal medical coverage, but if the system we have isn't working, where's the problem? Medicare is not a perfect system, but it works. It costs about 15% of the insurance company plans! Health care coverage should be managed by and practiced by doctors and nurses not insurance companies. Today, insurance companies and lawyers get more of your American health care dollars than the doctors and the hospitals.

The warnings about a single payer system emphasize the problems that can arise. No system can avoid all problems, and we have several examples of single payer systems that work. Canada, France, Cuba, Norway and Sweden all have systems that provide better coverage for more people at a lower cost than our current system. Shouldn't we at least give that a look? The opposition comes from those now in the dominant position. They stand to lose their current income unless they make their system more responsive to our national need. If they can, let them continue. If not let's emulate the one that works best. If we can follow the dollars and see where they go, we will get a picture of where the problem lies. But the operators of our current system keep those numbers obscure.

The primary reason that medical expenses get out of hand is because there is inadequate oversight. No industry serving the public need should be self-regulating. That puts the industry into a conflict of interest. Today, the insurance companies and the drug companies are in control—not the physicians. These companies were formed to help people, not to gouge them. Let's keep them on track, and get a universal medical insurance that we can all afford, and on which physicians will not have to pay $100,000 per year for malpractice insurance.

There is yet another problem with health insurance. If insurance companies, and especially Medicare and Medicaid pay for all the medical expenses, people will be very casual about using them. Got a sniffle? Go to the clinic! I recommend, as many companies do right now with co-payments, that every visit to a doctor costs the patient something. Not enough to prevent visits for serious ailments, but enough to prevent frivolous use of a system merely because it is free. $5 for Medicaid, and $10 for Medicare should be sufficient. One cause for expanding health care costs is that patients sometimes abuse it. Abuse is not a one-way street. Not all the blame falls on the insurance companies. A fair amount of it falls on ambulance-chasing lawyers who tend to squeeze the system for all the money they can get—deserved or not. Advertisements by lawyers claiming that they will get you a large settlement if you ever used a Guidant Pacemaker are outrageous. And some of it falls on patients who don't seek regular medical attention, but go to the emergency room when the problem gets out of hand. Making the ER your primary care center is enormously expensive and wasteful. The problem is complex and will require many solutions. But we should at least get started. Got a better idea?

It will take a multi-faceted approach to make universal health care effective and affordable. Hadn't we best get started?

CHAPTER 2
The All-American Aristocracy Tax

The very wealthy have devised a clever sound bite to entrench their favored position in our society. Calling the inheritance tax a "death tax" is a misnomer aimed at convincing the 97% of unaffected citizens that it is detrimental. It is a clever means for the very wealthy to pass assets to their heirs so the heirs won't have to earn their own.

America is the land of opportunity. Not because we pass our worldly goods to our children, but because we develop in them the skills to succeed on their own. A massive inheritance is an invitation to lethargy, and, sadly, most heirs to fortunes are lethargic. Does the name Paris Hilton ring any bells? It was a system of inherited wealth that created the American colonies, and nearly destroyed England. It was only the transfer of government power from the wealthy to the elected that saved England from self-destruction. That is why the House of Lords is largely ceremonial, and the House of Commons wields the power in England. Can you imagine Prince Charles at the center of the government in England?

Calling the inheritance tax the death tax is clever, but dishonest. If the chairman of Exxon Mobil dies leaving his $800 million estate to his heirs, he doesn't pay one cent in taxes. His heirs do. Why not? They didn't earn that money—he did. If he wants to leave something to his heirs, leave them an education and some skills and some goals. Prepare them to face the challenges they will face just as he met the challenges he faced.

Our wise founders recognized that and established the inheritance tax to make sure that opportunity came to those who earned it rather than inherited it. That's what America is all about. Eliminating the inheritance tax goes counter to our basic fundamentals. The argument that it destroys family farms or small businesses is an invention. They probably can't name five small businesses or family farms that were destroyed by the inheritance tax! If they can, there can easily be a special arrangement for operating business assets that operate as a unit.

Parents want their children to have a better life than they did. The problem is that they equate easier with better. Easier is rarely better. Don't take away from your heirs the opportunity to revel in accomplishing a difficult task that they doubted they could manage. The thrill of accomplishment is a far greater reward than the ability to receive or pass on assets. Help your heirs prove that for themselves.

In addition the inheritance tax exerts strong pressure for the very wealthy to establish charitable foundations which can escape that tax. That is another way of shifting burdens away from the government. We don't need the Aristocracy we fought to escape 230 years ago.

Finding fault is easy—finding a solution is hard. I propose that the inheritance tax be amended. For estates up to $1 million there is no inheritance tax. The next $9 million—25% tax. The next $90 million—50%. Anything over $100 million 75%. Charitable donations or foundations remain untaxed. Do you have a better way? I'd love to hear it!

CHAPTER 3
Political Campaigning and Reporting

Political campaigns are vital in a democracy. Ideally they inform voters about the goals and objectives of the candidates. I am disturbed by the recent trend in campaigns and in the reporting of them. The thing a voter needs most is what plans the candidate has for the future. After all, there isn't really much you can do about what's already happened. Of course people need to know what is going on and what the consequences of past laws and actions are. Even more important is what elected representatives are going to do about it. Those plans are remarkably absent from today's political campaigns.

I'm not talking about candidate's views of the utopian world they want to create. We all have those dreams. I'm talking about the hard work that needs to be done to get there. Calling the opponent a bad guy and pointing out his errors that are readily apparent in hindsight, is not a plan for the future. He rarely is a bad guy. He, like his political opponents, is a fallible human being who really believes in the goals that he presents. Besides, who in this world has lived to the age of maturity without making some mistakes? What is important is not that he has never made a mistake but that he learned from it and is better for it. My disagreement with him doesn't make him a bad guy. Realistically, I rarely disagree with his goals. It is his methods of achieving them that brings the conflict. If I can see his plan then I can decide if I think it can achieve those goals. But today I rarely see such a plan either in the campaign or in the reporting of it. Campaigns focus on problems, not solutions. Candidates mouth wonderful views of the end results they want to create, but not a word about how they will achieve it.

There is a reason for this. Finding fault is easy. Finding a solution requires you to dig into the problem and find the root cause. Then you have to figure out how to change that root cause to eliminate the problem without producing a mass of "collateral damage." That is not a simple sound-bite process. In the first place few problems have a single cause, and even if they do, those causes are usually intertwined with other factors. That is where the difficulty arises, and that is also where the differing viewpoints on the proposed solution will arise. That is as it should be. Most truly great solutions are achieved by cooperative effort that assembles inputs from diverse sources. The effective candidate plants the seed of an idea that gets developed into a solution. Candidates should propose <u>a</u> solution, not <u>the</u> solution.

TV ads and radio sound bites by-pass this complex process and present a one-sided view of the problem, and a statement of the goal. They don't have enough time, or effort, to present a plan that can be evaluated on its merit. In fact a large proportion of the ads don't even directly address the problem—only the bad guy who let it happen. Voters already know what the problem is. They don't need to be reminded. What they need is a plan to correct it—a much more challenging task.

Political ads today are designed to convince—-not to inform. The guy who pays has an objective in mind. Does this mean that our system encourages people to buy your vote? In a word—-yes. Each of us has a goal, but few of us can pay to promote it. Those who can, do. So the political "adscape" is dominated by money. But money merely makes ideas visible—not good or bad.

Think of it this way. If I spend a lot of money for a political ad, I want to get something for my money. Am I going to dwell on the problems or on the people who will be damaged or inconvenienced by what I propose? No. I will paint the rosy picture of what I want and convince you that it will help you too. Don't you believe it! There is always a downside, even to good legislation. Ads won't tell you about that. The person or organization that pays for the ad will be the one that benefits most. That's why many political ads don't say who paid for them, even though the law requires them to. The easy way is to form a new organization such as "Americans for Democracy" and have them, finance the ad. You and I don't know who Americans for Democracy is, but it sure sounds great.

The Campaign Finance Reform Act written in the late 1940's was a blatant effort to get around the prohibition of corporate donations to campaigning. (Our founders were pretty savvy.) It allows companies and unions to form Political Action Committees (PACs), which can finance and place political ads. Since its passage, campaign finance has increased fifty fold! How do you escape that problem? Ideally, repeal the law that is commonly referred to as the PAC law. However, we all know that will not be possible, because all the PACs will fight to retain it. So try this:

First: Limit the number of lobbyists to five or maybe ten times the number of legislators. There are over 100 today. There should be a substantial registration fee for PACs and lobbyists. That money should be designated exclusively for campaign financing.

Second: All hearings and debates upon pending legislation, whether held by an individual legislator or by a group, shall be announced in open hearings and shall include representatives from all sides of the subject issue.

Third: Establish federal or state financing of campaigns supported by PAC and lobbyist registration fees and public donations to a campaign finance fund.

Fourth: Require that half of all PAC contributions be used not for political campaigning, but for one of perhaps 20 or 30 diverse social organizations approved nationally to help all people. That might be called the SAC law——Social Action Committees.

The idea is to get money out of politics, or at least limit it so that it is not the overriding factor in a campaign. With the Internet and blogs, the word can get around in ways that it never could before 2000. Let's learn how to campaign on merit instead of money! I would also require, as part of their franchise license, that every television station supply a certain number of free political campaign hours to every qualified candidate during campaigns. (Within 90 days of an election, for example.) The air is public property, and should not be sold for political purposes. A true democracy cannot be purchased.

CHAPTER 4
Wind-chill—Whazzat?

The advent of the 'Wind-chill Factor" introduced in the late 1960's has caused more confusion than enlightenment. What in the world does it really mean?

The wind-chill factor is well named, but poorly measured. What it attempts to explain is the rate of cooling or "chilling" caused by wind. Although it may be convenient to equate this wind-induced cooling rate to the cooling rate of much colder still air (the wind-chill temperature) such a rating has little or no significance to people who have never stood out in the extreme cold. Claiming a temperature is other than it really is only confuses the public.

Wind chill deals with the cooling of a warm body, most significantly, your own. There are two major factors in how fast that cooling is—air temperature and the force of any air movement that blows away the heat and thus accelerates the cooling process. In still air, the layer of air immediately next to your body warms up, and helps insulate you from further cooling. Wind blows away the warm air and increases your heat loss. The current rating relates that increased rate to the rate for a still day of a lower "wind-chill" temperature. To say that the cooling rate (read wind-chill) is as fast as it would be if there were a completely still day of thirty below zero may be factually true, but is misleading. In the first place an absolutely still day is rarely if ever encountered. Further few people go skinny-dipping in the dead of a Vermont winter—they wear clothes if the expect to survive. When it is ten degrees out and there is a twenty mph wind, the cooling force applied to your warm body may indeed be equivalent to a completely still day of minus nine degrees, but that is entirely academic. Unless he is an ice fisherman who forgot his shack, no one will stand out in a minus nine degree day for very long. What's more if it's ten degrees out, there is no way you are ever going to get cooled to minus twenty. When you get to ten degrees there will be no more cooling. (There will be no more living either.)

I suggest a new rating for wind-chill. The entire reason for reporting wind-chill is to help prevent damage or serious discomfort to human bodies. Suppose you rated the risk of damage to your body in exactly those terms. How many minutes under the prevailing conditions will it take for your bare exposed finger to become seriously damaged by over cooling? That's an experience almost everyone has had once in a while. You want to make a short trip to the barn and get the snow shovel. You won't need any gloves for that short trip. Wrong! It is ten below zero and blowing twenty mph—your bare finger will freeze in about 3.5 minutes—one minute less than the trip to the barn and back through three feet of unshoveled snow. What's even worse is that you will pick up a shovel that is also at ten degrees below zero and it will greatly increase the cooling rate of your gloveless hands. You probably are at serious risk. If the wind-chill were stated in the minutes required to permanently damage a bare finger, it would be much more informative and would eliminate the confusion about "wind-chill" temperatures.

There would be another advantage to this method. Clothes are insulators. Like the insulation in your house, they can be rated by their ability to retard heat loss—called the R factor. Relating the time for biological damage to the R factor of your clothing will give direct information on what your risk is and how to reduce it. That's what you want isn't it?

For the future I would like to see wind-chill rated as the number of minutes required for serious biological damage to a bare finger followed by a recommended R factor for the clothing you wear. "Wind-chill is six minutes and R8 clothing is recommended." "Wind-chill is 2.5 minutes and R 17 clothing is recommended." Now, doesn't that warm your soul?

CHAPTER 5
Containment—The Crown Jewel of Prevention

Prevention—that's the key. We spend massive effort and resources establishing systems to prevent accidents from happening. We have security systems, safety devices, monitors and early warning systems. We employ teams of safety engineers who analyze every facet of risky operations and devise remarkable systems to prevent accidents. The systems they create avert untold millions of troubles and problems.

But accidents still happen. Pan Am flight 102 goes down over Lockerbee, Scotland. The Exxon Valdez spills oil all over Prince William Sound. Three mile island terrifies most of Philadelphia. Chernobyl pours radioactive dust all the way to Lapland. Are we wasting our time? Are the effort and the money well spent?

Yes, the effort is well spent and probably should even be increased, but it is clear that there is a serious flaw in this system. And the more sophisticated the system, the more serious the flaw. We assume that if the safety system is careful enough and we study all the factors, we can prevent accidents. If we do our homework, we can eliminate accidents—Zero defects! In fact Zero Defects was the fad in the late 70's and early 80's. The problem is that it was also unachievable. There is no such thing as zero defects! This is a contentious problem because there are sophisticated experts who believe that you can identify and control every possible source of problems. I suppose they are right theoretically. But practically there is no way!

If something can go wrong, it will. It is not a matter of <u>if</u>, but a matter of <u>when</u>. When viewed in that light it becomes obvious that having a failure plan is the most critical part of any prevention system. Almost all of the major disasters in history were disasters not because something happened, but because when it did no one knew how to respond. One of the most glaring examples was the Three Mile Island "Melt down". That nuclear power plant was superbly designed and had several levels of disaster prevention. In fact the system worked perfectly—except for one fact. There were people there. The first thing they did was to shut down the safety system. Had there been no one on the job, the reactor would have shut down and the incident would never have occurred. Here is a major system that was indeed perfectly designed but the operator had no confidence in that system and shut off the very system that was designed to prevent what occurred. It is remarkable that despite three levels of human error extending over a period of 72 hours, nothing really serious occurred.

But that fact was completely obscured by the fact that, because they assumed that the problem would not occur, they had no action plan when it did. They misinformed and antagonized the public and the governmental agencies that were charged with public safety. They terrified nearly 3 million people and panicked people who were in fact in no real danger.

The key to this and to other such problems, like the Exxon Valdez was that they had invested so much in the prevention system that they assumed it could never fail. In either incident had they presumed that a problem would occur at some date and had an emergency response plan at least 95% of the problems would have been solved.

So containment is the single most important of part any prevention system—the presumption that it can go wrong and a systematized plan to handle the results, minimize the damage and accelerate the corrective measures. Had Exxon had huge containment barriers and massive cleanup equipment available for immediate deployment, the overwhelming bulk of that oil spill could easily have been contained. Such containment barriers had been in existence for several years prior to the incident, but not in Prince William Sound.

By assuming that it was preventable Exxon allowed oil to flow out of control until it became too late.

Look at Chernobyl. That was a disaster on a scale probably about 10,000 times worse than Three Mile Island. Essentially all of it was because when the problem arose no one knew what to do. They assumed that it couldn't go wrong. When it did they were at a complete loss.

This problem is a basic human mindset. We foresee problems. If they appear to have serious potential for damage we, quite naturally, try to install measures to prevent them. That is as it should be and these measures protect many more people and things than we can even imagine. Most are thoughtful, carefully planned and placed with great care. The only flaw is that the safety engineer works in the belief that every contributing factor can be controlled. Usually he's right—they can be. But the practical fact is that they aren't. You can control 90% or 99% or 99.9% or even 99.999% depending upon how much you want to spend. But you cannot control every factor—-it is much more cost and time effective to presume it will go wrong and have an emergency correction plan. Such a plan will save more agony than the safety plan itself.

Look at New Orleans and Katrina. We knew in advance that we were not prepared for a grade 4 hurricane, but we put off and put off providing a disaster plan for handling it when it did come. You will note that the largest complaint about Katrina wasn't that we weren't prepared, but that we didn't know what to do when it did! There is some talk about the fact that we failed to prepare for a level four hurricane, but that pales into insignificance compared to the complaint about government inaction after the storm. We still have the federal, the state and the local governments arguing over what the other guy did wrong. But the simple act of facing the fact that there would be a failure some day and to organize a response would have relieved more agony and saved more lives than were caused in the storm itself.

Let us learn from our mistakes. Always include in any prevention plan a system for coping with its failure.

CHAPTER 6
Flaw Enforcement

A governor of Illinois placed a moratorium on the death penalty when 11 death row inmates were found to be innocent. Several other states also eliminated the death penalty either temporarily or permanently. Most of these were in response to disturbingly large numbers of convicts who were found to be innocent. Although this is pretty sensational, it is only a tiny part of problems facing our law enforcement system today. In Georgia an inmate remains in jail after DNA tests proved him innocent eight years after his conviction. The prosecutor says he'll stay there because the case is closed.

Miscarriages of justice are disturbingly frequent. One of the most disturbing aspects of this travesty is that the criminal justice system doesn't find the evidence to prove their innocence—citizen's groups and outside elements do. Our criminal justice system is bursting at the seams. It doesn't have time to look back and learn from its mistakes. In fact it doesn't have the resources to do the job right in the first place.

Is there something we can do about this travesty before we are all consumed by it? Of course there is. The concept is simple, but the practice is elusive. Focus on justice——a term rarely heard in courtrooms or police stations today. Police are trained to catch criminals, not to provide safe cities. In addition police are rewarded for catching the bad guys, not for keeping the peace. The problem becomes serious in our increasingly diverse society when the definition of "bad guys" becomes "people who aren't like me."

It gets even worse in the court system where overworked prosecuting attorneys are praised for convicting people, not for upholding justice. We have created a new sort of Roman Games where the ultimate reward is given for skills of persuasion, not for finding the truth. Clients flock to attorneys who win cases, regardless of whether they bring about justice. In fact, the most sought after are the lawyers who seem to be able to defy justice and win for a loser. If you already know the accused is guilty, why bother with all those small details and minor bits of evidence? Get the bad guy behind bars where he can't do any more harm. That frees you to go on to the next 20 cases that are screaming for attention. When there are more cases than they can handle, the easiest solution is to streamline the system and lock up those bad guys ASAP. But if prosecutors compete for the Olympic Lock-up Gold, who is left to protect society?

The system is not working. The United States locks up a larger percentage of its citizens than any other industrial nation. We have 2.5 million people in prison in the U.S. Does this make us a safer nation? No way! We have more homicides per capita than any other industrialized country by a wide margin. Our crime rate exceeds that of any other nation by a wider margin. It would seem that retraining our law enforcement personnel would be a far better way to spend taxpayer money than to lock up one out of every hundred people in the country. If we were to focus on "corrections" rather than on incarceration we would spend less money and have a safer society. This is a demanding process, and one for which it is extremely difficult to gain the political will.

Let's turn the current incarceration system on its head. Look at the three duties of our law enforcement system: Punishment, Restraint and Rehabilitation. Reverse those.

Rehabilitation, restraint and punishment. We call our jails "Correction Facilities." That is a misnomer. We don't have the resources to rehabilitate. It is assuredly easier to throw away the key, but it is neither cheaper, nor better. The main measure of a prison's effectiveness should be its recidivism rate. The lower the better, because it is then beginning to do its job. There should be two measures of the effectiveness of our "corrections" system. First:

What percentage of our citizens is in prison? Second: What is our overall crime rate in the U.S.? Those are the measures of success of any corrections system. If we were to focus on those, we would find our expenses would go down. In the past two decades it has gone up, and we are faced with building more jails to house ever growing portions of our populace. We are going the wrong way. We need a fundamental change in our system.

It's easy to blame policemen and prosecutors for the problems with the system of justice in America today, but they are not the real culprits. They are part of a system that has lost sight of its objective. This is partly because justice is not an easy thing to establish—it takes time and effort, two things in short supply in our overloaded system. But even that's not the whole reason. Americans have never come to a consensus on how to deal with unacceptable behavior. We demand three incompatible things of our prison system and the courts that support it. First we want to punish. Ah, yes, we are a vindictive nation. Next we want to restrain. This is a necessary step to protect society from its most violent elements. And, oh yes, we want to rehabilitate. But the system offers little or no help for the early offender to guide him out of the system and onto the path of "righteousness." Most of us seem to know who the bad guys are and could care less about how they got that way.

America has a long history of punitive justice. In fact, punishment may not be within our power to deliver. The basics are that different people have different ideas on acceptable or excusable behavior and a prison will not change that viewpoint. It may indeed show the prisoner that his views are at odds with the rest of Society, but probably cannot change his view.

A good deal of our present glut stems from drug laws that fill our jails with minor offenders while the manipulators behind them and who prey upon the uneducated and unemployable rake in untold profits. In our effort to free our country from the ravages of drugs, we have focused on punishing the user and his supplier. We fill our jails with people whose prime offense is trying to find their way in a society too complex for them to grasp. The dealer, who is inadequately educated to be employable elsewhere, is an expendable tool of the drug lord who is interested only in building an insatiable market for his wares. He has brilliant plans, which, like Napoleon's, can be carried out by the stupidest private in his army. This includes a sub-rosa advertising campaign of daunting effectiveness. Our drug enforcement system attacks the privates, not the plan behind them. We don't do much to curb demand—only to limit supply. But we should note that the percentage of our population that is incarcerated has risen to all time highs. This indicates that society is jailing the wrong people for the wrong reasons, unless we are to believe that this generation of Americans is inherently worse than its predecessors. When the numbers of citizens you jail increases more rapidly than the population it is time to look at the system, not the prisoners.

But it gets worse. We overload our jails—-facilities that are hard to build, harder to finance, and take endless political maneuvering to place. Faced with more prisoners than the system can handle, we establish early release programs, which are so indiscriminate that they release hardened criminals as well as minor drug users. Willie Horton helped defeat a presidential candidate, but we didn't learn. We still place hardened convicts on parole at immense risk to society merely because we lock up too many minor drug offenders. Are we really protecting society?

The district attorney in Georgia who holds an innocent man because "the case is closed" has clearly forgotten that he is paid by the citizens of his state to provide justice, not prisoners. He points out that a legally constituted jury found the man guilty. He neglects to say that they had insufficient evidence, or even false evidence. He's too busy with his next cases to face the fact that he made a mistake in his errant rush to judgment. He has too much to do to afford the time to look back. Besides, why would anyone who is praised for getting convictions want to admit publicly that one was a mistake?

When you train police officers and prosecutors to catch people, that's what they'll do. And if you reward them for jailing people they will get better at it. But that training often produces an "insider" attitude in the very people paid to protect society. It produces an "us against them" system that justifies its mistakes and considers outside controls as meddling.

On the other hand, if you train those same people to produce justice, that's what they'll do. And if you reward them for maintaining justice, they will get better at that too! This is a more difficult process and may overwhelm a system glutted with desperate dropouts who stray from a path they are not educated enough to master.

When I was a small boy I was taught that the policeman was my friend. If I had a problem he's the one I should go to for help. Can you imagine my horror when my children came home calling the police "Pigs"? The broadcasting of marijuana and the influx of ethnically diverse peoples put a strain on our justice system from which it has not recovered. Although it will not be cured by a simple review of its goals, it can assuredly change course and readapt towards the original goals—the ones that stress peacekeeping and stress helping limit-testing youths cope, instead of short-circuiting them to jail. There isn't one of us who hasn't made some pretty serious mistake in our youth. That's how we learn! When the system substitutes punishment for guidance it creates what we are trying to eliminate—renegades who are at war with the system and the society that supports it. Let's build a system that helps us get it right instead of punishing us for doing it wrong.

It is not enough to complain—that's too easy. The hard part is to come up with a better way. I'm not sure I can do that but I can certainly provide a number of steps in the right direction. Not being a law enforcement officer I have no real comprehension of the problems they face—but they do! Let them build on this beginning.

To start with, police all over the United States are currently held in low esteem and often feared by the very public that pays them. Of course there are shining examples of model police forces that serve their public superbly but today they are a small minority. So step one is to eliminate police. Replace them with "Peacekeepers." No the change in name will not by itself solve many problems, but it is symbolic of a total reorganization of the system.

At the beginning of World War II there were only about a dozen countries in the world in which the police were respected representatives of a friendly government. The United States, Canada, England, Australia and the Scandinavian countries respected police who kept the peace and were a part of a peaceful society. Throughout the rest of the world police represented a repressive government that wanted to control instead of facilitate social activity. There are large portions of the world where that is still true, including many of the largest cities in the U.S. Even today the word "Police" is more feared than respected in much of the world. Why not get rid of it? Even the name change will help change the character of the recruits it attracts. Violent types who are prone to the abuse of authority will find "peacekeeping" much less attractive than the SWAT Team.

Next, change the reward system. Peacekeepers should not be judged by how many criminals they catch because everyone they catch will be a criminal. I suggest that departments be rated on how many calls they answer and resolve with neither an arrest nor violence. Encourage the peacekeeper to help his citizens learn how to avoid conflict rather than to clap them in jail after a conflict has already escalated. Have peacekeepers speak in schools, but not on how they punish offenders, but on how to avoid the need for peacekeepers altogether. Responses that end up in violence after the peacekeeper arrives should bring a reprimand and a mandated review of better techniques.

Reward supervisors for training peacekeepers to avoid violence rather than to practice it. Physical restraint and threats of force merely teach the troubled citizen that violence is a valid way of solving his problems. Of course, force is required on occasion, but the job of the peacekeeper is to minimize it. The real winners are the ones who can avoid it altogether. Can't we have an award for them?

Finally, how do we treat prisoners? When a person is arrested he is confined to a cell and given special rules to live by that are vastly different from those of society. We are teaching prisoners to be prisoners, not citizens. They should be employed, have earnings and demands in jail. They should learn in jail how to live in a society they could not manage before they went to jail. Companies should be invited to have shops in jail where prisoners work, get paid and learn new skills. Since they are at some risk, they should get a slightly lower labor rate. That is better than hiring illegal immigrants. Then, when the prisoners get out of jail, they will be employable and will not have to return to those practices that got them arrested in the first place. The objective of a prison, aside from restraint, should be teaching prisoners how to get along in society, not jail. Recidivism should decrease by 75% or more.

Such changes are clearly not enough. But they are a start. They serve to refocus the prison employees on keeping the peace instead of keeping the jail. It will also help prisoners become respected members of society, rather than symbols of oppression. This country doesn't need more jails—it needs fewer prisoners. Americans may never agree on the proper objectives of a criminal justice system. But they will assuredly agree that minimizing the need for such drastic measures is better for us all.

I am sure that more knowledgeable people will have many far-reaching ideas on how to make local "peacekeepers" a step toward a functional society instead of a system of separating the bad from the good. Let's hear it! How would you make law enforcement an agent of growth and progress instead of a vindictive reaction to failure?

CHAPTER 7
Free Trade vs. Fair Trade

All countries rely upon trade with other countries. Over the centuries plans and agreements have developed that attempted to regulate such trade to the advantage of each trading partner. Of course each country tries to squeeze the most out of trade agreements, but the advantages swing back and forth so that usually each country gets what it wants from trade agreements. Today the U.S. depends upon two primary trade agreements: The General Agreement on Tariffs and Trade (GATT) and the North American Free Trade Agreement (NAFTA). These complicated documents address the problems of different currencies, different resources, different demands and different populations. They are designed to ease the barriers and restrictions on international trading. Each has had its successes in the past. All in all they encouraged world communities to trade with each other to their mutual benefit.

The world changes and these agreements need periodic revision and upgrading. Recently the globalization of the world economy has produced some glaring inequities in these agreements. The movement of goods has become much easier and the ability of companies to manufacture in one country for sale in another has become almost a standard of trade. Companies build plants in other countries, primarily to take advantage of lower labor costs. Many countries have policies that suppress their workers to the advantage of their employers. This "Imperialism" does indeed produce substantial price reductions in goods to the advantage of consumers everywhere. But it also creates a huge mass of poor and disadvantaged workers worldwide. In many countries this is a system of serfdom bordering on slavery. It produces a worldwide system that favors a few at the expense of many. GATT does not address these labor conditions, and thus contributes to this inequity. NAFTA lists as an objective the creation of new jobs and increased wages, but there are no regulations about either of those in NAFTA. NAFTA also lists environmental protection as an objective, but no regulations on the environment appear in the NAFTA. As a result, companies have been moving internationally with the assistance and support of repressive regimes in various countries. Slave labor is a common product of this activity.

It will be to the advantage of the whole world to address and eliminate these suppressive practices. The wealthy oppose such activity, and support governments that tolerate or even favor such repressive labor practices. But in the long run, they will benefit from more realistic labor rates as the market for their goods increases because better-paid workers are able to buy more goods. Henry Ford, back in 1910 said he wanted to pay his employees enough to be able to buy his cars. He used high wages and innovative manufacturing techniques to bring the price of his cars down—not up. That idea was key to making the automobile the prime mode of transportation in America, and now in the rest of the world. But most industries don't see it that way. They support governments that oppose fair labor laws.

That is a prime reason that South American countries call the United States Imperialists. We have consistently favored suppressive governments in South America. NAFTA could and should be a major force to bring South America into the 21st century. But there is strong opposition to such action from companies that benefit from the low labor rates imposed by foreign governments. But look at this. Why do you suppose there is so much pressure for illegal immigration into the United States? The people come here because they cannot make a living wage in their own country. Instead of supporting that, the United States that should be the driving force to change it. We need a revision from North American Free

Trade Agreement to North American Fair Trade agreement. Our own companies like Nike and Littelfuse thrive on the suppressive labor practices of other countries that oppose such modifications in NAFTA and GATT. That is short sighted at best and criminal in all probability. Why should a company president make $50 million a year because he pays his Mexican workers less than $2/hour and forces them to live in hovels with dirt floors and no water, electricity of toilet facilities? Neither can they buy a television set that uses Littelfuse products? A Nike shoe costs more than two week's pay.

When you go into Wal-Mart, essentially all of the goods you find there are made in China. They are made by workers earning less than one third of American workers, and American wages have already decreased. My 18-year-old television set recently died, and in an attempt to buy American I avoided Wal-Mart and purchased a Magnavox. When I got it home, inside where I did not see it at first, it says Made in China. So too my Kodak camera. This could not happen if we did not export our high tech manufacturing equipment for the use of those "peasants." For about twenty years unscrupulous American companies have been making huge investments in manufacturing plants in oligarchic nations, which suppress their workers for the benefit of the employers. Nike makes no shoes in the U.S., and builds plants in countries that suppress their workers. If the wages go up, Nike moves to another country abandoning their previous factories.

This practice makes us the primary support of China with over $100 Billion annually in trade surpluses. We have sent 3.5 million jobs to China in 5 years. In Mexico it is worse. We build plants to employ workers at $1.90/hour. That is better than starving with no job, but it is well below the U.S. wages across the border. So 11 million Mexicans cross the border illegally and suppress the U.S. wages. Instead of a dirt floor hovel for a family, they pack 40 people into a house with no electricity and send American money back home to support the family. This is bringing people out of poverty? That's the American way? Nike claims to be paying more than the "natives" are getting. Since they are otherwise unemployed, that's easy. The U.S. border employers, who employ illegal aliens, claim that Americans won't take those jobs. Not at $3/hour they won't. It is not the American dream to live with 40 other people in a house with no running water.

The amnesty people claim that we are cruel not to accept these poor waifs into our bosom and help them. But there is a limit to how much we can do. We already support China, which is not our responsibility. Need we also support Mexico and Guatemala, which aren't our responsibility either? The way to deal with Mexico is to make them support their own people instead of doing it for them. Do not support suppressive regimes in other countries. If we believe in fair labor practices here, why don't we believe in them in other countries? We need not tell them how to run their country, but we certainly can say that if they don't support their own people we won't support them.

I made a little calculation. The labor content of a small Littelfuse that sells for about 25 cents is 0.0238 cents. That is $1/1,000^{th}$ of the price of the fuse. If you tripled the wage to $5.70/hr. it would add 0.07cents to the cost of that fuse. Littelfuse couldn't even see the difference in profit margin, and some Mexican family would be able to buy a television set with Littelfuse components. They wouldn't have to cross the border illegally and work for less than minimum, wage in the U.S. Who gets hurt?

NAFTA needs to be replaced by the North American Fair Trade Agreement. It must contain anti-slave labor and environmental provisions with import restrictions or tariffs on goods made that way. This can be a tool for raising the living standards all around this hemisphere. And, although it will doubtless reduce the company's profit margin it will probably increase their overall profits by increasing the market for their products.

CHAPTER 8
Ancient Garden Mystery Solved—Almost!

Not long ago when I was ethnic-cleansing my garden—I was struck by the answer to one of my most persistent problems—one that many a gardener before me has pondered for millennia. Why is it that all the grass seed you plant in your lawn fails to grow, but in the garden that you weed, it grows profusely? The answer was suddenly as clear as gin. The seeds "Transgerminate." They determined that the place you, the warden, planted them was wrong! That is no place for any self-respecting grass. The proper place is forty feet away on the garden. Look at all the attention and good fertilizer that is available over there. Why should grass waste its sweetness on high traffic areas where it will assuredly be trampled unmercifully and beheaded as soon as it begins to make any headway? So grass will take root over in the garden, and not where this martinet garden freak has tried to blight its life. So by the process of transgermination, all the grass seed you spread in the lawn takes root in the garden many feet away. The soil is loose there and captures moisture. Weeds and other competitors are rigorously discouraged. Fertilizer is often applied to stimulate the grass' innermost desires, and that nasty beheading device is forbidden there.

"Unlike my warden, I cannot move once I put down my roots. So why put them down in a neglected wasteland? It is clear that no plants can live here or he wouldn't need to put seeds here in the first place. Answer? Transgerminate! Take root where you like it best! One might even surmise that it would be better if the warden didn't want you there, but that may be a little prejudicial."

Now some of you skeptics may think this is going a bit far. Plants have no long-term plans. All they do is grow. Plants can't think. Don't you believe it! Why else would our most virulent weeds grow up through the very roots of your most delicate flowers? I'm not sure all plants are vindictive but they are all greedy. They want the best. The greediest are called weeds. They are the unplanted ones that do better under constant assault than the flowers on which you lavish loving care. But none has perfected the art of transgermination better than grass.

Transgermination explains some related mysteries of gardening. It explains why weeds never get blight—they won't take root where the blight is but root somewhere else instead. It explains why during droughts the unplanted residents survive while their nurtured neighbors croak. The survivors have transgerminated to the spots where water and nourishment are most accessible. Yes, the art of transgermination over millions of years has become finely tuned.

I know I need more research into transgermination. I have yet to find the physical mechanism by which plants accomplish this feat. Could it be akin to teleportation? Nor have I found out why Night-blooming Cereus can't transgerminate. But it is clear that transgermination is widely prevalent. By what other mechanism could a pad-leaf orchid appear on a mountain trail two miles from its nearest relative? These further questions will assuredly succumb to more intense research. I was so excited to discover this long-sought phenomenon that I rushed into print before I completed my studies. I am thrilled by the thought that, after years of fruitless search, no future gardeners need ponder these mysteries. I would appreciate input from all quarters. Assuredly, now that I have discovered the key process, others far more experienced than I can help unravel the full details of this widespread but obscure phenomenon. I am willing to admit that I have not found the mechanism behind transgermination. Can you?

CHAPTER 9
Illegal Immigration

Illegal immigration into the United States is not as simple a problem as it appears. It is complicated by the globalization of our world. If we are to discuss policy, stopping illegal immigration is simple. Immigrants come here illegally because they are so badly suppressed in their own countries that almost any risk is worth getting here to make enough money to survive. If we want to stop illegal immigration, what we need to do is remove the incentive. Enforce existing laws against hiring illegal immigrants. That removes the incentive and will stop the flow. Fences and border patrols will not.

But policy cannot be separated from politics. That is where the problem arises. There are people and businesses that have a vested interest in hiring illegal immigrants, because they can underpay them and increase their profits. If we were to enforce our current laws, they would have to pay minimum wage to those people and increase their cost of production substantially. They will scream that they cannot compete with foreign goods which are made with slave labor elsewhere. They have a point.

But look at the larger picture. Globalization is desirable because it will increase the standard of living everywhere. That will put buying power in the hands of people who cannot buy anything today. It will increase world consumption, world commerce and world opportunity. But in the hands of a few greedy corporations and the politicians that they support, globalization is an opportunity to greatly increase today's profits by capitalizing on the labor of suppressed and underpaid people all over the world

So how do you get American companies to compete with slave labor in other countries? For many years we were creative in our development of labor saving devices that markedly improved productivity of American workers. We could make products in the U.S. for less with $10/hour labor than other countries without that advanced technology could make with $1/hour labor. That is what made the U.S. the industrial giant of the world. We all grew together. Our standard of living far outpaced other nations. We were far-sighted enough to see that paying our people well expanded our markets as we expanded our Gross National Product.

What happened? There were a few bad guys that tampered with that plan. But there were myriad contributing participants who were shortsighted and greedy and wanted to squeeze more out of the economy in which they lived. They were more interested in increasing their share than increasing the whole pie. And they did. Labor unions, for example, opposed every labor, saving device that industry created, because they saw it as a way of decreasing jobs and decreasing their membership. They didn't see that those labor saving techniques allowed their workers to make $20/hour instead of $5/day. They were more interested in increasing union membership than in helping the members they already had. They saw fighting with management as their prime objective.

So what did industry do? They began moving their manufacturing overseas. And they found a bonanza. Instead of using the devices to help foreign workers earn more money they kept the wages low and enriched the corporations with larger profit margins. Executive pay went from 30 times the average worker pay to over 500 times in many companies. But our American politicians kept supporting those repressive governments, so the trend to go overseas and capitalize on the misery of the poor grew out of hand. We exported more and more of our technology so that corporations could be more profitable at the expense of foreign workers instead of with the cooperation of our own. We were exporting more and more of our jobs overseas where suppressive governments kept wages low and corporate profits high. In the process we made China into the manufacturing dynamo that America was in the early twentieth century. But we lost sight of the fact that well-paid workers <u>are</u> the market. So, of course, more and more of those goods came back to be sold in the United States and our trade deficit began to skyrocket. No one else could afford to buy the products, so they are sold here. Instead of working to increase the world's standard of living, we artificially kept it low in producing countries. So, of course, our own followed suit. U.S. wages began to decrease, as we competed with slave labor elsewhere.

This is a one-way street. As our trade deficit increases more and more U.S. dollars find their way overseas. Soon we found that foreign countries own increasing percentages of our corporate and national debt. We have become a debtor nation. In the looming fiscal crisis we may be at the mercy of foreign money interests. In addition the pressure of unregulated foreign imports from slave labor nations have depressed our own wage scale. We gave away the technological advantage that allowed us to be more productive with high cost labor than other nations could with low wages. So, despite increasing inflation, wages have been stagnant in the U.S. for two decades. Adjusted for inflation, the average wage has decreased in the U.S. in the last twenty years. Congress refused to increase the minimum wage. However, they raised their own eight times. Corporate executives, relying on foreign governments and their repressive wage policies, have become extremely wealthy. We have more billionaires now than we had millionaires in 1900. And we have more poverty too. Is that what we want? It's great for the billionaires today, but what about tomorrow. The net result is that globalization has brought the world to the lowest common denominator, instead of the highest. We are sliding down to the standard of living of the poor countries instead of bringing them up to ours. And there's the problem. After General Motors runs through its U.S. resources and goes bankrupt, a new GM will be thriving from its new headquarters in Bangladesh. And the poor shall inherit the earth.

It is easy to find fault, but hard to find solutions. That is particularly true when politics enter the scene. There are a number of things that can be done to reverse this risky trend. But, while policy is easy, politics is hard. First we must stop the hiring of illegal immigrants. That is easy to say, but politically difficult to accomplish. Corporate interests will oppose such a move and will bring up dozens of reasons why that is a bad idea—"Can't compete with foreign manufacturers", "We pay higher wages in Rwanda than Rwanda does."—etc., etc. They will spend advertising dollars to make all those shortsighted and specious arguments look attractive—or worse to make it look like we're hurting their illegal employees, or practicing racial discrimination. We must not let them mislead us. Remember—a well-paid worker is a buyer, but an underpaid one isn't.

We must also change the NAFTA and other "free-trade" agreements to "fair trade" agreements. Such agreements will impose serious import taxes on foreign goods that are manufactured with starvation wages and environmentally destructive techniques. Our industry spokesmen say that the illegals do jobs that Americans won't do. That is patently false. The truth is that Americans won't accept starvation wages and poverty living conditions. Illegal immigrants often live in squalor and send most of their money back home to support their starving families. They are bleeding our resources back to their homelands. Meanwhile we school their children and provide health care for them. We are educating South America's children for them. We should bill those countries for that service that their own countries will not supply. We need not do it free. Of course they won't pay, so we take it out of their favorable trade surplus.

And that brings us to the biggest political nut of all. We must not support repressive foreign governments. We must deal with them, because they are sovereign nations, but we need not support them. We can reach out to help them bridge the gap between slave labor and decent wages with technological advances but not at the expense of their workers. We have a long history of supporting repressive regimes in other counties around the world, particularly in Central and South America. This creates an enormous flood of unpaid or underpaid people into the bountiful United States. It is not our responsibility to employ those who can't find employment in their own country because of repressive regimes. Mexico encourages illegal immigration and hasn't made any effort to stem the tide. It is easier for Mexico to unload its poor on us than to solve the problem. But we have supported regime after regime in Latin America that create the poor who pour across our borders. While our people are supportive of oppressed people all around the world, our government is not. It is our non-government organizations that do all that good work—not our government. If our government really believes in democracy, we should stand up for democratic principles everywhere. This goes far beyond supporting foreign elections, which are more often than not rigged, unfair and controlled by the powers that be. Support true democracy and ignore or minimize our dealings with autocratic and repressive regimes. That will be a major shift in our foreign policy—one that we are led to believe we have already done, but which in fact we have not. Think of the dozens of despot dictators whom we have supported in the past, including Peron, Betancourt and Saddam Hussein. In a remarkably short time those newly democratic nations will see that a well-paid working population is a mass market for goods. Sure, prices will go up, but not as much as wages.

Prices are going up anyhow. But the increases are going to giant corporations who pay their executives $180 million per year, not to the workers who make all those goods and only want enough to buy what they make. In this country our middle class is resigned to the fact that it takes two working parents to support a family— an almost unheard of situation in the forties and fifties. Lee Iacocca worked for Chrysler for two years for a dollar a year. It didn't seem to cramp his life style. I suspect Chrysler shareholders wish he was their CEO again even at a large salary.

Solutions aren't easy to find. But they are harder to carry out. It will take much determination on the part of every citizen to accomplish what should be obvious to all. We will not overcome government and corporate short sightedness by sitting back and feeling picked on because our vote "won't count." Of course it won't if you don't cast it. Democracy is a marvelous form of government, but it is a participatory one. If you don't participate, you will lose it, and corporations that can't vote will continue to buy votes with misinformation and misleading statements that support their shortsighted greed. This problem will not go away. It must be driven away. Do we expect someone else to do it for us?

Write, or E-mail your Congressman! Demand fair trade and enforcement of immigration policy. Don't listen to the blurring of illegal immigration with immigration and racial discrimination. Immigration built this nation, and is a good thing. But illegal immigration merely saps that power and sends it to other repressive regimes in totalitarian or despotic countries. Our fair trade and our immigration policies are inseparably joined. It is complex, but manageable. But it won't happen until you speak out and demand it. If you really want to see a better future, get involved. Because if you don't, General Motors will create a better future for GM and GM executives. Is that what you want? If not, let's hear your ideas on how to do it better. Your future may depend upon it, and your children's future will!

CHAPTER 10
Home—The Educational Dropout

When this country was founded, essentially all of our education occurred in the home. As schools arose they were primarily religious schools and the bulk of our education was still delivered in the home. That was appropriate for the day when 70% of society lived on farms and the skills of life were applicable to every facet of daily life. But with the industrial revolution, the percentage of farm-raised people dropped dramatically from about 70% to around 3%. The skills of life tended to become those of the factory, not the home. Schools were redesigned to cover that gap.

But we failed to recognize that this change was essentially moving the educational responsibility from the home to the school. Homes gradually dropped out of the schooling process. For a long time we developed PTA's and PTO's to provide guidance to the schools. But many of the home things just dropped out of the educational system altogether. On the farm, even the four-year old had daily tasks like feeding the chickens or carrying the water. If they didn't gather the eggs, there was no breakfast. We have come a long way to make the life of the child easier—but not better. Four-year olds have no responsibilities at all today. In fact in many homes teenagers don't either. Our school year is still designed around the farm structure. We only demand 180 days of school from our kids, because years ago, they had to come home to work on the farm during the summer months. School stops at 3:00, because farm children had to come home to do chores. Today they come home to an empty home, if they come home at all. Both Mom and Dad are working outside the home, if there is even a Dad at all. They have no demands. Idle hands are the devil's workshop, so we have developed an enormous drug problem. Parents aren't around to guide and direct their children. We have a frightening number of drug addicted people almost every one of whom became addicted before they were 16 years old, and the age is getting younger. This is a major dilemma in today's family life, but few parents feel responsible for their children's addiction.

These are the problems of an outdated school system, which addresses problems faced a century ago, but fails to address the problems of today. We need a drastic and comprehensive remodeling of our schools. They aren't producing a quality education for our children who rank 13th in the international educational ratings of the world.

But let's not blame the schools. Public schools have severe budget limitations because people don't want to pay taxes to support them. Neither do parents go to the schools to help them or guide them. Our schools do not fail us so much as we fail our schools. When was the last time you went to your children's school and tried to get something changed there? When last did you participate in school guidance meetings or PTA meetings? Do you know what your child's grade point average is? What is his worst subject, and have you helped him understand that subject? What kind of grades do you expect of your children?

Let's take a look at the demands upon children today and revamp the school to serve those demands. Children face an increasingly complex society. Educational demands are always growing. Jobs require ever better educations, but even more, jobs require employees to take responsibilities. Do our schools teach responsibility? Do schools present independent studies that require students to find out, on their own, the background and requirements of a specific project? One hundred and fifty years ago a sixth grade education qualified you for about 80% of the jobs of the day. Today a college education or post secondary training course is required for over half of all jobs. But the graduation rate is declining in this country. Did you know that almost 30% of college students are foreign born in the U.S., and nearly 60% of graduate school students are foreign born? In addition, nearly 30% of incoming college freshmen require remedial training in at least one subject. That, in itself, must tell us something about our public education system. And, in the inner cities, the high school drop out rate is almost 60%. That paints a pretty bleak picture of our future.

But let's not be glum and depressed. Here is an opportunity for us to remake our public schools to be the best in the world as they were in the mid 20th century. Here are some ideas, but these are neither the greatest nor the only ideas. These are actions aimed at specific problems. The reason for this paper is to stimulate your ideas and, yes, your action to remake our nation's schools. The future of this whole nation is at stake.

The most important first step is to figure out how to get parents involved in schools—not just the schools, but with the education of their children. That is a lost function of today's home. I don't believe it is possible to run a superb school without parental involvement. That is a primary advantage that private schools have over public schools. Parents, who want to have their children well educated, not only spend the money, but the time to assure that it happens. So how do you inspire a parent with a sixth grade education to help with the tenth grade education of her children? Shouldn't the schools have several parents' nights throughout the year, when they come with (or without) their children to the school for an update and a chance to review progress versus goals? Make it attractive with benefits for the parent as well as the children. Have a parent-catered dinner or potluck. Give student awards that night. Involve the parents in the planning of those events. Make school involvement a rewarding experience for the parents as well as the children.

Perhaps we could have two to five weeks in the year when the school week is Tuesday through Saturday, and have the parents come on the Saturday.

Probably even more successful is to require a course in "Parenting" in every high school. If teenagers learn the needs and functions of parenting, and learn how to apply and use them they will be much more active when they themselves are parents. Such a course should be taught in ninth or tenth grade, when such issues first begin to cross the minds of maturing students. I would like to see that as a statewide requirement. I suspect that such a course would also sharply reduce the teenage pregnancy problems we face.

One of the biggest problems schools now face is the problem of illegal, and illicit drugs. The prime reason for this is that the students aren't challenged enough. They have too much free time, and no serious demands upon them. This is hardly the way to prepare them for the ever more competitive job market they face as foreign students with better education apply for the same jobs they do. I think every student in eighth through twelfth grade should have an out of school assignment that they must complete to advance to the next grade. I think that the school day should be extended an hour every day. This cuts one third of the idle time out of a vulnerable youth's day—one in which she is not prey for a drug dealer. This will not go over too well with teachers, who have plenty on their plates already, but the out of school project could be assigned during that hour. That hour is already filled for many students by organized athletics as baseball, football, basketball, soccer, swimming and track teams train. But for the non-athletes and the nerds, there are many projects that could be productive as well as instructive. Schools should make sure that every student has some outside activity, which places demands upon them between 3:00 and 6:00 PM. Students today have essentially no demands upon them and are given a strong sense of entitlement that they are not required to earn. Is it any surprise that most are totally unprepared for their first job?

Our nations kids are falling behind in academics as well. We are thirteen in student achievement worldwide. Why do we demand 180 days of school while Chinese students are required to have 220? Schools are still honoring the farm boy who had to be working in the fields all summer. Instead we now have a big vacation. School should start in August, and continue through June. In addition, students seventh grade and above should have a project for the summer—a project that they have to plan, organize and complete on their own. Let them see the difficulties of scheduling and coordinating. At least one of those projects should require working together with other students.

There is yet another problem, which schools exacerbate rather than alleviate. Most children are in day care, or pre-school by the time they are three. Two working parents can't be home supervising kids all day. So children today are learning at three what I learned at five in kindergarten. Since that is already the rule, let's make it official. Start formal education at three, not five. That has another great advantage. Studies show that learning capacity maximizes at age three, not five. We are neglecting the most valuable learning years that we have. We are adding brain cells at a maximum rate at three, and many of those cells will atrophy and disappear if we don't challenge them. Don't let them get away! We add brain cells all our lives, but never as fast as at age three. Challenging those cells puts them into the brain in an active role, and they stay with us for life. If we don't use them, they never get activated, and soon dissipate. I suspect, but cannot confirm, that such early education programs could increase the ultimate IQ of individuals. It's worth a try.

But that leaves us with a cost problem. I can't pay for 12 years of school, how will I pay for 14? The answer is "Don't!" Have students graduate at age 16, not 18. Rework our curriculum so that school goes from age 3 to 16 instead of 5 to 18. As we have increased the education demand, we have also delayed the age of independence. But at the same time we have had a steady increase in nutrition, and people mature a year or more earlier than they did in 1775. So now we have people who are sexually mature at age 12, but not financially independent until they are twenty—an eight-year gap. In 1775 the numbers were 13 and 16—a three-year gap. And so we see greatly increased sexual activity before independence is achieved, and the out of wedlock birth rate has exploded. If we cut the age of independence back to 16, it would sharply curtail that. Remember, the age of getting a drivers license is already 16, as is the age of legally dropping out of school. If we graduated at age 16, that would enormously decrease the number of under educated adults that can't find or hold a job and become drug dealers.

But few 16 year-olds are ready for college (That may change if we institute this plan). But they are qualified for holding a number of jobs. Why not require a year of public service? That will answer another of our current social problems—lack of interest in the social workings of society. 16 year-old graduates should be required to take a job in military service, the government, at an NGO or in social or charitable services. They should be paid minimum wage and learn to balance a checkbook, even though they are still the legal responsibility of their parents at age 16. Switzerland has had a similar program for three hundred years.

There is one more thing that has escaped both the school and the family. Even in presidential election years only 55% of eligible voters vote. In other years it is 45%. We have seen what this lack of interest in elections has brought us in the past thirty years—-a government that is responsive to big business and pressure groups rather than to the people. A democracy is participatory, and students should learn that as early as practical. It might solve another national problem as well—voter registration. We heard a lot about problems with voter registration in the last two elections. Your graduation certificate from your class in voting could well be your permanent voter registration ID. It would follow you everywhere when you moved to new jobs in other states. But learning the dynamics of voting, and the importance of every vote would bring home to everyone the basics of democracy and how you must be aware of and involved in the process. If we don't act like a democracy, we soon will not be one!

CHAPTER 11
Mary Jane

The debate over legalizing marijuana for medical purposes is truly pointless. The answer stares us all in the face every day, but we don't want to look. Marijuana is one of many substances that induce artificial feeling of joy. I use the terms artificial because one of the great things about human life is the thrill of accomplishment. There isn't one of us who hasn't had the thrill of accomplishing something they doubted they could, or that they thought might be impossible. You won a race, or solved a problem or created a new device. These "highs" are an integral part of a productive life.

Man is ever searching for easy routes and artificial highs are a common pathway. These are the "highs" that occur not because of something accomplished, but because of a substance introduced into your system -one that creates that feeling of joy when success has not been achieved. The thrill is there but the accomplishment isn't.

The problem is that the artificial high route has unintended consequences—many of which are undesirable or harmful. Undoubtedly, the biggest artificial high industry is the liquor or alcohol industry. The world is plagued with the unintended consequences of the alcohol industry. Worldwide, the largest single cause of fatal automobile accidents is alcohol. Alcohol addiction is a serious international problem consuming billions of dollars every year. Lives are ruined, marriages destroyed and jobs are lost every day. This is the price we pay for trying to get the thrill of accomplishment without the accomplishment. Many of us wonder if it is really worth it. The facts clearly demonstrate that it isn't. But the pattern is established, and the laws are in place. It is entrenched in society and will not go away. Man will continue to pay the outlandish cost of this artificial high.

Sometime in the last 100 years smoking marijuana became an accepted artificial high. It has grown to a major industry, but without the legal acceptance that applies to alcohol. "Pot" is discouraged by most governments and is illegal in most places. Despite this, "pot", or "grass" or "weed" is everywhere—as are the unintended consequences of its use, or should I say abuse. Marijuana is well entrenched.

Now comes another facet to complicate this practice. Unlike alcohol, there are medical benefits from marijuana that have value in clinical use. And, of course, we have many marijuana users who want to make it legal so that those medical purposes can be fulfilled—or at least that is what they say. So the challenge is to divorce the medical use from the recreational use.

That is a relatively simple challenge. It is no surprise that medical benefits have been found for marijuana. We have an enormous drug industry, which has grown from the early discovery of medicinal benefits from various natural substances. The industry has taken a chemical approach and carefully investigated the chemical causes of these benefits. They have chemically altered them for even greater benefit. This is a long and demanding process and has produced "miracle drugs" that do remarkable things for the ailing human body. This applies to marijuana as well. They have discovered that tetrahydrocannabinol (THC) is the active ingredient in marijuana that produces the desired benefits as well as the desired high. This provides an easy answer to the legalization problem. Let us put a prescription version of (THC) on the market. Prescription drugs are assigned by a qualified physician to relieve or cure specific symptoms and their causes. That would leave the pot smoking to the recreational and frivolous user. It will take some legislative backbone to enforce that distinction, because the pressure to get it the easy way, by smoking pot, will have many loud and active supporters. In fact there are already many supporters of legalizing marijuana. In California, which legalized smoking of marijuana on a prescription basis in 2004, the abuse has far exceeded the use. Big surprise! It will continue to do so.

It is a simple thing to just say no! There will be no prescription for smoking pot. There may be prescriptions for THC by injection, by mouth or by inhaler, but smoking pot will remain illegal. It has been shown clinically, that marijuana smoke is more detrimental to the lungs than tobacco smoke. Why take that risk? The drug industry should love that, because it will give them another drug on which to make profit.

It is worthy of note that every society seems to need some sort of artificial high. As far as I know, no society or culture has failed to find and use one or more. Modern society has accepted alcohol as its legal high. If that choice were to be made today I would personally strongly favor marijuana as the legal high instead of alcohol, since I believe that is has far fewer and less damaging side affects—the unintended consequences. Pandora's box is open. Don't open another one.

CHAPTER 12
Taxes and Population Growth

In the last quarter of the 20th century it became apparent that the population of the United States was beginning to strain our vast but finite resources. Please note that this is not just an American problem, but a worldwide problem. America was founded on the idea that bigger is better, and so we continue to push for bigger things and bigger populations. Nothing goes on forever, and it would be sad for such a compassionate nation to find out that it had already exceeded the sustaining capacity of our 50-state terrain. Also note, that despite the immense increase in world wide population the world is the same size it was 3 billion years ago, and the same size it will be 3 billion years in the future if it lasts that long. Such a cognizant nation can surely look forward to the day when population increase is a detriment—not an asset. No one knows when that day will come but assuredly with a population that doubles every 36 years it can hardly be many centuries in the future. The concern is that it may already have occurred!

Of course technological advances will expand our capacity and will tend to relieve that strain, but there is no way it can eliminate it. Doubling a population every 36 years will create enough people to convert every organic molecule in this world into people in less than 500 years. That will leave no organic material for food, for trees, for animals, for grass or for new children. How does science cope with that?

Long before that fateful day life will become so constrained by shortages of life's necessities, that human life will be more greatly devalued than it is in Iraq today. People will be forced to make life or death decisions about their fellow man. Are we up to that? Do we want to doom our great grandchildren to such a fate?

Now is not only the time to think about it, it is time to do something. If we do so now, we can wisely avert that disaster with almost no strains on our society. I propose a first step:

The Internal Revenue Service currently provides tax deductions for children. Although this deduction has been around almost as long as the income tax it has varied considerably. Congress cannot let any money matter alone even for an entire two-year term. As I write this the deduction from taxable income for each child living in your home is $3200/yr. That tax relief is a donation from the IRS to help you provide for your children. There is no constitutional mandate for such a deduction. It is a benevolent act by the much-despised IRS. I propose that we make one simple change in that deduction. We should provide a $3200 deduction for the first child. But we provide only a $1600 deduction for the second child. For the third child we provide no deduction. For the fourth and all succeeding children, we reduce that deduction by $1000 each.

This scheme leaves control with the parents—where it should reside. No one is penalized or punished for anything. We merely make it economically advantageous for families to have two or three children. This is a relatively small economic advantage but it will work.

The People's Republic of China is the only nation that has taken any serious steps toward population control. They have a one-child policy which is not really enforceable, but which puts painful pressure on families throughout that nation. Although I disagree strenuously with the action they took, I admire China for having the courage to face the problem and take action. I suspect that their policy will change at some time in the future, but I doubt that it will disappear altogether. It is time for the United States to face the problem. It is time for us to do it right.

We are not the first nation to face this problem. The Mayas in South America had a vast and complex society of approximately 50 million people. But they cut down all their forests and so overstrained the resources available at the time, that they had many internal conflicts and territorial battles. These became so bad that by the time Pizarro arrived in 1515 they had already decimated their population to 5 million. Pizarro assuredly added to the demise of that culture, but he was by no means the cause of it. It was already under way. Shall we follow in the footsteps of the Incas and the Easter Islanders or the Greenlanders like Haiti is doing today? Shall we fight so much internally that Kim IL Jung shall have an opportunity to destroy us?

CHAPTER 13
Are Schools Outdated?

Our public schools have been overwhelmed with change. Their basic curriculum was created not long after the civil war when about 75% of students were headed for a life on the farm. Today less than 3% are aimed at farms which no longer even resemble the ones of 1880. There have been enormous changes in communications, in technology, in diversity, in social structure and in goals. These are tremendous challenges to schools—challenges with which they need our help. So far we have added and changed bit by bit, responding to the changes as they occurred. Not much attention has been paid to the basic structure of the school and its curriculum.

The changes have become more rapid. We have had more change in society since WWII than we did in the previous 80 years. Communications have been totally revised—from hand-written papers to television, the cell phone and the Internet. Schools have not yet capitalized on these innovations as teaching tools. Television is probably the greatest teaching tool ever invented, although the Internet may well surpass it. It can bring images and discussions to students from all over the world. But it has been so dominated by commercial interests that we are teaching 13 year-olds about erectile dysfunction instead of the violent conflict between dominant religions. The Internet is a remarkable communication tool, but schools don't yet capitalize on it in their classroom assignments. Why don't we demand some use of Internet search engines in some of their classroom assignments. The school libraries all have banks of computers for use by those students who don't have such access at home.

Even the ages of school children were set by the demands of farm life—A far cry from today. 65% of families have either one parent, or two parents that are working outside the home. In 1865, the home was the farm, and a parent was always available on short notice. As a result, about 70% of today's kids aged three to five are either in day care or preschool, things that didn't even exist until after WWII. They are learning at age three things that we learned at age five. Why not make it formal and start public school at age three?

Then we face the other end of the school years. Because of better nutrition and better medicine, children mature sexually at between 11 and 13 today—as opposed to 13 or 14 after the civil war. But the increasing complexity of society doesn't educate children sooner, but later. We have more than doubled the time between sexual maturity and financial self-sufficiency. Look at the results. Almost 30% of children today are born out of wedlock. Many are born to children who are themselves not yet fully educated or self-sufficient. Having a child usually stops or severely limits a person's access to education. This is creating a serious social stigma. We aren't educating our children. Almost 30% drop out of school before they complete high school. This is in a day when a college education is almost a requirement for a productive life. We have created a serious educational disconnect. It's time we closed that gap. I suggest that the curriculum for schools be aimed at ages 3 to 16, instead of 5 to 18. Prepare kids for self-sufficiency as soon as possible. I suspect that the teenage pregnancy rate would drop by 60% under such a plan. I'd like to see it decrease by 100%

But how many 16 year-olds are ready for college? Few if any. I suspect that most 16 year-olds can't balance a checkbook, or their credit card account. Here is our opportunity to build our society. We should require one year of community service of all kids before they get their high school diploma. That could involve a wide variety of such service. Military, charity, Non Government Organizations (NGO's), government, even the schools themselves. That is where they would learn the value of cooperation. Teaching the young the value of responsibility provides a major contribution to a self-sufficient life. They must all learn self-sufficiency some time; why not make it a part of their formal education? They should be paid, probably the minimum wage. They are still under 18 and are still their parents' responsibility, but they could and should learn the value of earning a living. A low wage will assuredly instill in them a love for the education that will allow them to increase it. It will also help teach them money management—a skill missing in a large proportion of our young. They should be required to open a bank account and keep track of their expenditures. They will be contributing to a family income while learning to make it on their own. How do they intend to pay for the college that is becoming ever more a requirement for living? Perhaps some of the wages paid should be credit toward college tuition. Challenging our kids, will make them better people. Coddling them will make them vulnerable.

CHAPTER 14
Prisons—Our Failed Resource

The United States has struggled unsuccessfully with our prison system for centuries. It is about time we took a close look and convert this financial rat hole into the resource it could and should be.

Americans have diverse and conflicting opinions about our prison system. Most of us see it as a system for punishing offenders. Some of us see it as a system for restraining dangerous people who have a potential for doing harm. A few of us think of prison as a place to rehabilitate the offender so that he will not repeat his transgressions. There are also a few who think of prison as a place to dump all those undesirables and throw away the key. No prison system can serve all those needs—they are in conflict and incompatible. What we should have done is to analyze those many objectives and serve those we can and abandon those we can't. In the long run that will be the only way to keep costs in control and to produce anything of value from this beleaguered system.

Sadly, punishment is not truly an option for prisons. If a prisoner is convinced that he was either right or justified in his unacceptable behavior, no amount of prison time will change his mind. He will continue to feel picked on and mistreated, and in all likelihood will repeat his offensive performance if the opportunity arises. If, on the other hand, he believes that he made a serious mistake and was wrong to do so, no amount of prison time will change his mind about that either. His remorse is already achieved and lengthy incarceration will almost certainly make no improvement. Sentences of thirty, forty or fifty years will not serve any great purpose. The ability of a prison to punish is clearly limited. The most important objective is to prevent recurrence. Jail time will not do that after it has been completed.

Some offenders have adopted an unacceptable way of life. They are repeat offenders and show little or no inclination to change. If these people remain a threat to society they must be restrained from contact with it. For the safety of the general population, restraint is necessary and is a task prisons can perform admirably. Restraint of dangerous individuals is the function prisons can perform best out of all its diverse requirements. Restraint is very probably long term, although the rehabilitation of individuals inside prison is a desired objective.

Most prisoners get their first incarceration early in life. It is a sad fact that many first offenders, aside from being young, are neglected, uneducated, and unskilled. Their offense is frequently a desperate move to make up for their lack of skills or ability. The common drug dealer, who is a major portion of our prison population, has no skills, no job and no income. Drug dealing is a simple matter requiring little or no skill. It produces income otherwise out of reach for those with little education and no job training. These people mostly fell through the cracks of our education system, often with the help of neglectful parents and similarly unskilled peers. Here is where the prison has an opportunity to supply what the over-wrought education system failed to do. Many prisoners are neither incorrigible in their evil ways, nor remorseful about their offense. They are simply unprepared to find other means of self-support. If our prison system has no other goals, it must assuredly fill in where school left off. Here is an enormous pool of undeveloped talent, which may well be converted to productive labor. Of course no system will be able to rebuild the lives of all of its members, but even if we could rehabilitate 30 to 60% of our young unskilled inmates it would be a boon to society and a great reduction in the financial burden of the prison system. Schooling should be an integral part of incarceration.

Instead of forcing prisoners into a caged way of life, prisons should be made as much like the outside world as possible. Lead the offenders into socially acceptable habits and into productive skills. If a prisoner serves his time and leaves with no more skills than he entered he will be a repeat offender by default if for no other reason. Prison terms should be based on the time required for the prisoner to learn a saleable skill and learn acceptable social behavior. Release from prison should depend upon the prisoner's ability to cope with and succeed in the real world. Once that is accomplished, further time in prison serves no purpose and adds greatly to the cost of the system as well as the frustration and bitterness if its inmates. Further, if the prisoner can't support himself in the outside word, he should not be released until he can. Sentencing should include such allowances.

The current term "Corrections Department" is a misnomer. We do not correct unacceptable behavior. We establish a closed community with different rules and different goals from the outside world. Instead of teaching prisoners how to get along in society, we train them in another set of standards, which will not help them become useful citizens outside the prison walls. What do we expect of them when they get out?

Of course there will be some prisoners who will not accept this retraining. They will become repeat offenders. If we do our job right, the existing recidivism rate should be cut to half, or less. For those who have never had a chance to experience normal societal living, prison should be a sample of how that is done. They should have jobs (including job training) in prison on which they can earn money. When they do so they should also pay some measure of rent as a model for their return to society. Perhaps they could earn certain privileges within the prison confines to help in the concept of goal setting. They should have social interaction on which they can develop community skills. Even if we succeed in only 30% of the cases, that would solve our current prison overpopulation problem. We don't need more prisons——we need fewer prisoners.

Many companies would be happy to farm out a portion of their production to prisons where they could get a favorable labor rate and perhaps even a source of future trained workers. They should be encouraged to do so.

This utopian view of prison may sound a little far-fetched. Perhaps it is, but the major barrier to that plan is ingrained preconceptions of the purposes of prisons. There are still those who want prisons to be a closet into which we throw all the dregs of society and forget them. This new idea will have to be sold and sold effectively. But if it is, the pay-off will be a smaller less expensive prison system and an increasingly productive society. When prison populations grow drastically as a percentage of the general population, as ours have in the past 20 years, it is a signal that we are doing something wrong. Let's take this problem and turn it into an asset. You have nothing to lose but expenses!

CHAPTER 15
Interrelated Problems

Combining problems can sometimes create solutions for all of them. Countries usually face multiple problems. Finding solutions that not only work but also can be accomplished is quite a challenge. But many of our problems are interrelated, and looking at the whole scheme of things can often find a solution to several at once. I have an exceptional example of such a group of problems, which just beg for a common solution. Try this!

Global warming is at last a recognized problem. The whole world is facing some very serious weather and related problems if we don't take some pretty strong action. But nations, being what they are, keep calling for the other guy to make the first move. Most nations blame the United States, because we are the greatest polluter of our atmosphere. But we are not the only polluter, and in a few years we will no longer be number one. China has already surpassed us in greenhouse gas emissions, and India will pass us in the next decade. So each of us points a finger at the other and continues his wasteful ways. We fight and blame and do little or nothing. We set ridiculous goals, like reducing our CO2 emissions 20% by 2050. If we were really serious, we could do that by 2012—and all the data shows that we should.

But we have other problems with China and India. We have an enormous and growing trade deficit with China, which manufactures cheap goods with slave labor and miserable working and environmental conditions. In addition China is beginning to challenge us for sources of energy. As a country that imports about 60% of its energy needs, we are increasingly at the mercy of countries that want to extract as much money from us as they can. It doesn't bother them if we have a recession or can't afford to feed and clothe ourselves as long as we keep buying their oil. (The proceeds of which, by the way, support terrorists.)

Make no mistake, when we run out of money they will treat China the same way—as long as they have the oil for which China is building a demand. (That may be far shorter a time than they now believe. Oil reserves are seriously overstated)

Does anyone see a solution to the two problems combined?

The United States has been working on alternate energy for over 50 years. We have developed a great deal of science that can make us energy independent, but almost none of that has been reduced to practice. The technology lags far behind the science. It has always been easier to just buy more oil and let the alternatives wait.

If we were to make a major national effort to produce alternate energy resources, such as wind, solar, hydrogen, geothermal, nuclear, tidal, river and ocean currents, we could solve our oil dependency problems and global warming within a decade. It would also create hundreds of thousands of jobs. What's more we could go to China and offer to help them along the same route, thus decreasing our trade imbalance, and giving us more in common with the worlds largest nation than in conflict with it. Being in a cooperative state with China will help both countries. Like it or not, China is the world's largest population. Although we dislike the "Communist" government of China, they have done wonders for that population in the past 30 years. They are becoming daily more democratic and less and less totalitarian. Why not give then a hand? We have nothing to lose but a potential competitor and possible enemy, and will gain a balanced trade partner at the same time.

Would any of you want to go to China and sell windmills? How about solar panels? Or hydrogen generators? The Chinese would love it and we would cut back our trade deficit. It might even give us an opportunity to get them to have better labor laws, so we can have a fair trade with them instead of an imbalanced one. Helping China come into the 21st century would be a boon to our economy as well as theirs. Any takers?

There is a hidden agenda here. That is involvement. We all read about alternate energy, but none of us does anything about it. We somehow think that is General Motor's job, or GE's. But it is my job and your job. We will not solve our problems by letting someone else do it. We need involvement—involvement of everyone. If we do it right, everyone will be a winner. If not, we will probably all be losers. What is your plan?

CHAPTER 16
Racial Balance

We have gotten into many hassles recently about "racial balance." It is particularly true in colleges and universities. But since the abolishment of slavery in the United States, the real goal has been to create a colorblind society or, put in different terms, a meritocracy. Although this appears to be primarily an issue with African Americans it surely does not confine itself to them. Latino Americans and Asian Americans face similar problems because, try as we may, we have created neither a colorblind society nor a meritocracy. That is a worthy goal and perhaps one that may actually be achieved eventually, but not within my lifetime.

The idea of racial balance goes counter to that goal. Instead of eliminating racial bias, in favor of merit, it uses racial bias as a selection method. It is ridiculous to expect every facet of society to have equal representation among all the races (or sexes). We may not like the idea, but races do have characteristics. These include natural differences in talents and bents. I don't hear the Al Sharptons and the Jesse Jacksons demanding racial balance in our football teams or basketball teams. I didn't hear Martin Luther King talk about racial balance. If a race has a peculiar talent, be it basketball or nuclear science let us capitalize on it. There was a tribe of Indians in New York City that built most of our bridges, because they had a peculiar ability to walk fearlessly and effectively on high beams and girders. Should we have demanded racial balance?

Jesse Jackson and Al Sharpton may indeed have a legitimate complaint about providing equal opportunity to the various races in education and perhaps housing. This is a symptom of a badly misguided educational program in much of this country. This can and should be corrected, but we have not been either very good at it, or very focused on the goals. No Child Left Behind is a wonderful name, but that is all it is. It punishes schools for poor performance, instead of helping them. Bussing children to other neighborhoods is disruptive and ineffective. Inner city schools need financial as well as instructional help. That should be the primary focus of our efforts to rebuild our school system. Instead of building charter schools outside of the neighborhood, we need to build good schools within the neighborhood. That is an achievable goal, but it is rarely accomplished.

If we truly want a colorblind meritocracy, we must really focus on achievement and opportunity. Of course some lines of work will have substantial racial imbalance, but if that is caused by racial characteristics, so be it. Different facets of society will have different racial balance reflecting the peculiar capabilities of one race over another. Many years ago the telephone industry switched from having men as operators to having women, because the industry discovered that women had a peculiar talent for answering the phone and directing calls. There was no outcry for gender balance, it just happened. During WWII women were recruited for manufacturing because the men were at war. But LO! Women were better at production line tasks requiring repeated operations than men. So, until we did that electronically, women became the mainstay of production line production long after the men returned from war.

Racial differences arose because different people lived in vastly different climates and circumstances and adapted to those conditions. If those racial differences produce a specific advantage, or disadvantage, don't decry it, but capitalize on it. Society may be racially balanced, but every facet thereof should not be. Let us learn to use the talents the human race has developed to the advantage of everyone, and let us learn how to encourage and grow those talents. In such a meritocracy, color, religion, sex and race won't even count.

CHAPTER 17
The Trouble with Shaving

Gillette hates me. I never use shaving cream. They would long since have gone bankrupt if they had to depend on people like me. Now how did I get into such a state? I am not a bearded outdoorsman, but what is referred to as clean-shaven. What? Without shaving cream? No way!

My father taught me to swim before I can remember. I spent almost as much time in the water as in the air until I was in fourth grade. One of the problems I encountered was wet hair. This is wimpy stuff, wet hair. It softens up and gets almost unmanageably limp. I learned to comb it wet, and as it dried it took on a little body and kept its shape—sometimes.

When it came time to start shaving, I noted that razors often raise havoc with your skin as they try to decapitate the little whiskers that are poking through. So I thought, "If my hair gets soft in water, won't my beard?" So instead of using shaving cream, I used warm water with a little bar soap. Marvelous! It gets pretty slippery, and assures that all your whiskers are soaking wet. I've never had a "razor-burn" problem since. I now realize that shaving cream emphasizes the cream, but minimizes the water. That's exactly wrong. Maximize the water and use just enough soap to assure that the beard gets wet, and that your face is slippery—even slipperier than with shaving cream. It's cheaper too! I don't even have to use after-shave lotion.

There is a side benefit too. I end up with a sink full of soapy water. It is there that I rinse the razor—not under the faucet. Razors get dull less because of erosion, (being worn away by whiskers) than by corrosion (being rusted away). Steel razor blades can and do rust under the stimulus of water. But soapy water is alkaline. Alkalinity in water seriously inhibits rust and corrosion. So your razor stays sharp at least twice as long.

You people with electric shavers might think about that too. The electric shaver shaves dry hard whiskers. That's bound to have an effect on your skin. Many years ago I tried using an electric razor. (My father-in-law invented the Remington electric razor, and prodded me a little.) My face immediately began getting raw and sore and even broke out in a rash. The problem disappeared when I returned to my water-based shaving plan.

So if you want a comfortable and a close shave, remember— water softens the beard and makes shaving it a breeze.

CHAPTER 18
Gas Rationing

Few people doubt that we need energy independence. But almost no one has a plan to achieve it. Oil reserves are declining and there is no amount of drilling that will change that. The response of the oil industry to high fuel prices is outrageous. They want more money to explore more ways to further entrench us in an unsustainable dependence on their oil. There is a better way. Former President Bush said we were at war. Since only Congress can declare war, that was not true. However, Congress did vote him extra powers under the War Powers Act. One of those powers is gas rationing. It worked wonders in WWII. It could make people think of alternate means of transportation as well as alternatives to gasoline. If gas is rationed, hydrogen and ethanol will become un-rationed alternatives. Public transportation will become a serious consideration. Car-pooling will become a good practice. Bicycles might be used more. How about walking? These last two might even attack our national obesity problem.

I recommend issuing gasoline and diesel oil rationing stamps for only 98% of the current usage. Do not ration alternatives like biodiesel, LPG, ethanol, electric or hydrogen. The pressure to develop these limited resources will increase. There should be no government money available for oil drilling. That money would be reserved exclusively for developing alternate sources of energy. The market pressure to buy fuel-efficient cars and trucks will grow exponentially. We would create thousands of jobs in alternate energy. Considering the job losses in the past decade, that result alone would be worth the effort.

Don't stop there! In the second year, issue stamps for only 96% of the current usage. In the following year, issue only 94%, etc. Since the demand will be decreasing, prices should go down, not up. In addition, biodiesel and ethanol may eventually be rationed also because they are both carbon-based sources of energy. In fact biodiesel produces the same amount of CO_2 per energy output as gasoline or diesel oil. But ethanol produces twice as much, because it is made by fermentation, which produces as much CO_2 as ethanol before you even put it in your gas tank.

How do we pay for it? By increasing the gasoline tax. Not a lot, but enough to pressure us into alternates. The additional tax dollars received should be exclusively devoted to clean alternate energy sources, such as wind, geothermal, solar, photovoltaic, nuclear, tidal, ocean currents, or hydrogen.

We have used more oil than we have discovered in each of the last thirty years, so oil companies should be charged a depletion tax rather than given a depletion allowance—this is a national resource, not a corporate resource. New automobiles should have a horsepower tax as well as a pollution tax—say $50 for every horsepower beyond 100 HP.

The response of the oil companies baffles me. Even sixth graders know that we are going to run out of oil. All these new wells and drilling sites will only delay the process and probably not very much. If the oil companies start developing alternate fuels, they will still be in charge of the future energy resources just as they are today. If they don't, someone else will. How can such a seemingly intelligent industry be so short sighted?

The oil industry says we can't do anything about oil prices without paying them subsidies to make more oil available or open the Alaska National Wildlife Refuge to oil drilling. This from the most profitable industry in the country? Who are they kidding? When was the last time they built a refinery in the U.S? I wish it were kidding, but it is a serious rip-off by a few power brokers who want to enrich and entrench themselves without a thought for our people, our country, or their own grandchildren.

The oil industry says we can't do anything now. Assuming a single solution put in their hands, that is true. But the oil problem won't be solved by a single solution. It will be solved by many. Gasoline rationing will pressure us to develop alternatives so we can make significant progress right now! Consider this. Every time the price of a barrel of oil goes up, the oil companies' profits increase. What is their incentive to keep oil prices down? With gas rationing and a gradually decreasing limit on oil imports, the price of gasoline would head for $1 per gal. rather than $6 per gal. And consider this. Fuel oil costs 20 cents more per gallon than gasoline. This despite the fact that fuel oil is more abundant, less refined and has no 20 cents per gallon road tax. That is the altruistic action of the oil industry. I would shed crocodile tears if the socially unconscious oil industry fell onto hard times because no one wanted their products any more.

The oil companies and the coal companies have established .org websites to inform people of the choices in energy and fuel. Have you looked at any of those sites? They are infomercials for the status quo of the industry. They don't give much in the way of information, and what they do give is entirely one-sided to favor their current positions. They talk of creative new ways to find and drill for oil— not on how to develop other energy resources. The coal site discusses pollution entirely in terms of SO2, NOx, mercury and arsenic. They neglect CO2 completely and fail to note that we have had technical solutions to those other problems for over 60 years! (I lied. The term sequestering does appear on the website without explanation of what it is or any method for achieving it.) They would be better off to spend that money in developing the alternate fuels that our great-grandchildren will have to use because the oil will be all gone. Meanwhile how will they explain their position to the millions of Floridians whose homes will be under water in fifteen years? How do they justify paying the retiring president of Exxon $400 million while Joe Workingman can't afford to fill his gas tank?

Legislators are terrified of even mentioning gas rationing because they think the public will vote them out of office. Have they tried? The public is remarkably savvy, and if they get the complete story, they will vote for a sensible solution to the energy problems. I suspect gas rationing will pass with flying colors.

CHAPTER 19
One Iraq?

America is involved in a worldwide debate over Iraq. In fact we are the prime player in that debate. Many of us debate get out or stay there. Neither is right! There are many doubts about how we got there in the first place. We all want to point fingers at someone and place the blame. That is a worthless endeavor. How we got there is no longer important, because we can't change that. What we do now is the issue. Most of us aren't even approaching it. It is far too complex for a quick answer, and it is beyond a quick fix. We need to look at the situation in depth and determine how to balance the many conflicting objectives of the people involved—not primarily the Americans, but the Iraqis and their neighbors. Stability, which appears to be a prime objective, will not be achieved by outsiders. There is a cultural conflict that can only be resolved by the cultures involved. Americans and other outsiders can help and encourage, but we cannot resolve that conflict. Let's try to look at this incredibly complex problem and draw some plans and actions from what we find.

Is Iraq really an entity, or an unholy alliance of battling factions assembled in 1920 by uninformed outsiders who wanted to prevent the reformation of the recently destroyed Ottoman Empire? Shiites and Sunni's had been fighting since the death of Mohamed's grandson in 687. Forcing them to live together in 1920 was no more successful than it is today. But the problem has gotten worse because, since 1920, we have discovered oil in that part of the world and it is unevenly distributed among combatants. We hear that the Iraqis want a stable Iraq, but is that really so? The Sunnis want a stable

Sunni state, and the Shiites want a stable Shiite state. But each sect defines Iraq in terms that exclude the other sect. We worry about a civil war in Iraq but we already have one. And it is not 5 years old, or 35 years old, or 85 years old. It predates us all!

The problem with "get out or stay" is only a superficial stab at a much deeper problem. There is such chaos there today that the area is a breeding ground of discontent. Egotistical mullahs and are brainwashing the extremely young population (the average age is 19) into factions primarily designed to advance the personal desires of the mullahs and ayatollahs. What they seek is dominance—-not peace. It makes one wonder what the definition of infidel really is. Neither the Shiites nor the Sunnis deny either Allah or Mohammed. Who, then, is an infidel? Americans are infidels even though by and large they believe in Allah (under his translated name God). So, the power hungry clerics are further subdividing the warring factions creating chaos.

That is only the basics. Now we add the Kurds to the mix. They are a displaced fragment of the old Ottoman Empire that also has ties to other Kurds in other lands like Turkey, Kurdistan, Syria, and Tajikistan. Upon that superimpose the power-hungry leaders of Iran, and Syria. It gets worse! We have to finance all that conflict with oil, which is unevenly distributed and much coveted by the parties involved.

Is there a way out? Perhaps, but not without recognizing the complexity of the situation. To resolve the problem, we should at least attempt to satisfy the needs and desires of the local people. Should there be separate Sunni and Shiite states? That's what the Shiites and the Sunnis want. Why do we know better than they do how to live in Arabia?

Ah, if only it were that simple. Democracy cannot be imposed from without. It is fostered from within. We have a bunch of egotistical tribal wannabes trying to dominate the area. They are more powerful than we want to admit. The trick is to give each of their egos just enough of a boost that they can live with the results, but not let one dominate enough to inspire bitterness among the contenders. And, a very big AND, how to distribute the oil money?

It is clear that what we are doing in the whole Mideast, and most particularly in Afghanistan, is not working. We must recognize that the Israel situation is directly connected to all this chaos. These are ancient tribal concerns that trump the more recent nationalist thought processes. Israel, and our unreasonable support for it, is a key factor to all this. We won't solve the problem until we take that into account. We must make Israel a viable neighbor instead of a predatory one. Israel has been brutally suppressive of non-Jewish minorities not only in Israel, but in the surrounding lands including the Gaza strip. Israel has a powerful minority that believes that all that land was given by God exclusively to them. And therein lies the problem—exclusively. Those people have shared that land, bitterly and resentfully for four thousand years. There will never be a winner, nor should there be. The best we can hope for is that they continue to share the land, but stop fighting for dominance.

So, our course is to neither to stay nor to abandon project. There is no black or white solution. Our job is to show them all that they can live together better than they can fight to eliminate the other. That same solution applies to the Sunnis and the Shiites. The action is to change the approach to one tailored around the complex needs of the local people. Soldiers are not nation builders. This is not a military problem. It is a cultural one. The opposition has chosen the weapons of war. Instead of responding with our own well-planned response, we have followed their inappropriate lead. We have gone down to their level of action instead of bringing them up to ours. Replace many of our soldiers with some experienced nation-builders who can then be supported by a smaller military in an exclusively peacekeeping role. We will not eliminate the need for peacekeepers until we begin to understand and ameliorate the needs of the local people and resolve their cultural conflicts. There must be a massive effort to promote tolerance and understanding among the clashing factions of Islam. But we live on the edge of the greatest revolution in communication of all time—the Internet. It is everywhere—even in Iraq. So is the cell phone. So far these remarkable new tools have been used against us more than by us. WHY?

I am old enough to remember Radio Free-Europe. It was a widely dispersed information network that had almost as much to do with the winning of World War II as did our military. It showed Europeans how to get along and how to resist their German oppressors. Look at Europe today—-a better society than they had achieved in 3000 years prior to World War II. That is exactly what is needed today in Asia Minor. A few power hungry clerics are indoctrinating huge numbers of young and uneducated youths into petty territorial and sectarian conflicts that will never be won and will perpetuate internal strife. If we want a stable Iraq and a stable Mideast, we must help them understand how to get along as they have, uneasily, for millennia. We need a massive radio, TV, Internet and cell phone TRUTH campaign to educate a deprived youth. It takes more maturity than exists in that mass of uneducated youth to realize that people who disagree with you are neither wrong nor bad, just different. That is certainly within our ability to teach. We don't have to sacrifice our soldiers to do that.

We must not do this alone. We are not neighbors of Iraq or Afghanistan. The Syrians, the Iranians, the Turkish, the Saudi Arabians, the Kuwaiti, the Pakistanis and the Jordanians are. Until we bring them all together and reach an agreement, there will be no peace in the Mideast. Impossible? No more so than the current course of action, whose sole goal is short-term stability. How about long-term stability?

We face a serious problem in the education process. Islam, more than many other religions, tends to revere the cleric as the guide and the leader. It is very difficult for Muslims to question the teachings of their local mullahs and ayatollahs. How do you convince an indoctrinated youth that his religious leader is off track—even when he is? We need some strong cultural guidance, perhaps from our own Islamic community within this country. Can they be convinced to counter the egotistical religious warlords of another country? It may be obvious to us that Moqtada el Sadr is killing more Muslims than infidels, but how can we make that apparent to his followers? An "Internet Free Mideast" patterned after "Radio Free Europe"may be the answer. Have we even tried to create one?

CHAPTER 20
Now Hair This!

Hair is strange stuff. Originally designed to keep bodies warm, it has gone off on a few tangents and serves many other purposes. One strange tangent is its disappearance from the domes of men. Perhaps that happened because men are so hotheaded that they need to be cooled instead of warmed. Regardless of its origins or purposes, it is a fact of life and we have a whole industry established for the exclusive purpose of combating baldness—like baldness is an evil thing. This industry has had its ups and downs. It is extremely creative. Noting that baldness is less than one thousandth as common in women as in men, someone had the idea of using women's hormone, estrogen, as a cure for baldness. This produced many undesirable and even risky results and was abandoned primarily because it didn't work.

Now the human body, like that of other mammals, is remarkably adaptable. It responds to demands. If you lift weights, you will get stronger. Exercise will make you healthier. Lifting weights will make you stronger. If you take care of your body, it will take care of you. Considering this, I noted that the top of the head has less physical contact and exercise than any other part of the body. Maybe the hair just got bored and felt neglected. So I decided to give it a little exercise. Every morning in the shower I vigorously scrub the top of my head with my fingers. I wanted to stimulate the hair roots so they no longer felt abandoned. And LO! The hair responded. It made a measurable comeback, and appears all over my once sparsely populated dome. Unfortunately, I took up this practice late in life and many hair follicles had already croaked.

Had I started at age thirty, I might have had more success, but I am pleased with the results.

Perhaps this is a lesson in life. Living things were created to accomplish things. If a creature feels needed, it strives and thrives. If it doesn't, it withers and dies. So while you stimulate your hair follicles every morning, stimulate your purpose in life. If you have goals and are going somewhere, you will be much happier and healthier. Try it. You'll like it!

CHAPTER 21
A Plan for Iran

Mahmoud Ahmadinejad and Iran are challenging the world. They are ramping up their nuclear refinement industry to the dismay of many other nations. Of course, they claim that this is exclusively for electric power. Since they are an oil rich nation that can produce electricity from oil for less than half the cost of nuclear power, the rest of the world is skeptical. Of course Iran has a right to develop nuclear power sources. The nuclear non-proliferation agreement, which they signed, allows that. So most of this conflict is based on distrust, rather than actual data. Even the non-proliferation agreement requires regular inspections by the International Atomic Energy Administration (IAEA), which Iran does not allow. There is much basis for distrust.

We can make a great case for NOT developing nuclear weapons. Who has it helped? What has any nation gained through nuclear weapons since Hiroshima except expensive headaches? We could easily show that that effort would be foolish and will detract effort from other important national goals. Join them and work together for better international relations and for eliminating the need for nuclear weapons. Threats will not cause anyone to disarm.

Other nations tend to offer the stick more than the carrot. We predict dire consequences of unknown ilk and threaten sanctions. Iran already has an unemployment rate of 25% and it is growing. How could we hurt them with sanctions? Furthermore, there is reason to doubt that an actual attack would ever be launched except by some rogue nation. Since the United States listed Iran as a member of the Axis of Evil and attacked its neighbor, Iran could well have some serious concerns.

Ahmadinejad is an egotist, with illusions of power. But he is losing support among his own people because he has failed to deliver on his promise of economic prosperity. I propose a way for him to gain the world status he seeks, eliminate the threat of nuclear proliferation and employ his people so that the promised economic prosperity comes closer to reality. Consider this: Anything that can be concentrated, like uranium, can also be diluted. Rather than make more nuclear material, Iran might take the current oversupply of weapons grade nuclear materials (93+%)and dilute them to fuel grade (83-90%). Iran already has the equipment to do that. Then they can sell fuel grade materials to the 400 nuclear power plants of the world at a profit. They will reduce the oversupply of weapons grade material, which is insufficiently guarded and at risk of capture by militant despots. They will employ their unemployed and increase their own prosperity. Instead of being a renegade, Ahmadinejad will be a local hero as well as gain international respect. He will be contributing to world stability instead of threatening it.

Having an idea is far from having a solution. I propose that the United States buy excess weapons grade nuclear materials on the open market. They will register them with the IAEA and, under careful scrutiny and control, sell them under contract to Iran for dilution to fuel grade material. This can then be sold to nuclear power plants worldwide, and Iran will be paid for their dilution efforts. Iran must allow close inspection by the IAEA, which must keep careful accounts of all such materials. A single slip and the supply is cut off. There should be a very tight control of exactly how much nuclear material is in Iran at every moment. No weapons grade material goes to Iran from any source until an equivalent amount of fuel grade is shipped out. The world will be utilizing the nuclear materials they already have rather than making more. We have too much already.

One of the consequences of this program is that it will increase the amount of nuclear power generated worldwide. It will also increase the nuclear waste problem.

Nuclear waste is a growing international problem. Consuming nuclear materials to make energy creates two general types of radioactive waste. High-level waste, which is fissionable heavy metal, can often be reprocessed to make nuclear fuel. Low-level waste, however, is not reprocessable and is substantially more radioactive than nuclear fuels. It is a radiation hazard, not an explosion hazard. This problem succumbs to the same technique as weapons grade materials. We can dilute them down to the same level of radioactivity as the uranium ores from which they were originally obtained. Then return them along with a few thousand trees to those same mines as a restoration project.

There is no doubt that nuclear power industry can be made as safe as other power resources. (It is already safer than coal even with Chernobyl.) But people were frightened by Three-Mile-Island and Chernobyl. Both of those incidents were preventable and, had there been sufficient personnel training, would have been. The nuclear waste remains. Iran can gain further status and employ more people if they dilute the low level nuclear wastes back to the radiation levels of the ores we spent so many billions of dollars enriching in the first place. Most mining industries are now required to restore the land they mined. Why not uranium mines? This could further employ Iranians and further increase the status of Mahmoud Ahmadinejad at home and abroad. What's to lose?

CHAPTER 22
Torture of Prisoners

The national debate about allowing the torture of prisoners completely misses the most important aspect of this gruesome practice—does it work? Study after study shows that torture does not bring more truth—only more talk. Why even consider abandoning one of the foundations of our democracy for an unproven technique? Why should we show the rest of the world that we don't really believe in our democratic principles—we just want them to? Is that the way to convince the world that democracy is better? We claim to be trying to establish democracies in other countries. Why not show them how well it works?

People who study interrogations do know techniques that extract more truth from prisoners. They do not involve torture. They do involve complex and difficult procedures that invade the personality of the prisoner and entice him to tell the truth. Going the torture route is merely a way of putting interrogation in the hands of unsophisticated flunkies who aren't knowledgeable enough to penetrate the natural resistance of prisoners to expose their plans or co-conspirators. Successful interrogation requires highly sophisticated techniques. It is not a simple matter to be practiced by amateurs. Torture is a short cut that falls short. It does not get the desired results. Please note that our entire Mideast conflict arose from misinformation. Why invite more?

CHAPTER 23
Tax Reform

Our country is spending more than it earns. We are living beyond our means. In this age of credit card debt and interest only mortgages, that seems quite reasonable to many. No matter how you look at it, the day of reckoning will come sooner or later. The sooner the better, because today we can cope with it, but if we wait long enough we won't be able to.

Of course, cutting the spending is a major approach to the problem—but only half of it. We have already spent beyond our means long enough that we can no longer tackle the problem merely by cutting our expenses. We have certain obligations that are already beyond our income and are still growing. Social Security and health care are two that come immediately to mind. They are each still growing, and demographics indicate that they will continue to grow. We will be forced to look at the income side of the pay as you go concept. If we wait too long we will exceed the income potential. Our grandchildren will live in a failed society that literally can't pay its debts—our debts, not theirs.

That brings up that horrible word—taxes. But if we want to continue our lifestyle, we all know that eventually we will have to pay for it. The bill is called taxes. Now taxes are a curious thing. No one likes taxes, but we all pay some. We do it because we know that we are paying for our lifestyle with taxes. We don't talk about that and don't want to admit it, but inside we all know what taxes are. Most of us complain about taxes. But surprisingly, the most common complaints are not that they are too much, but that they are too complicated. So a plan that simplifies taxpaying could easily gain support. The second most common complaint is that they are not fairly distributed over the extremely diverse income ranges. There are more complaints that the rich are under taxed than that the poor are overtaxed. Those who are served best by our society are far less inconvenienced by taxes than those who are served least. The current system gives special treatment to those who need it least, not most.

Income taxes are a major source of government income. There are individual income taxes and corporate income taxes. Complexity is not the prime problem with corporate income taxes but very few individuals can cope with the overwhelming 12,000 pages of the individual income tax code. Even their lawyers and accountants are sometimes stumped by this intricate delusion. It is time to admit that it is far too complex and needs a complete rewrite.

To begin with, income is income. We now have about 12 different kinds of income. Earned income, capital gains, income from trusts, inheritance, sheltered income, unearned income, etc. All of it is income. When it comes to the bottom line, the source shouldn't matter. It should all be taxed as income. That's what it is!

We have a sliding scale of income taxes. Starting at about 10% for taxable family incomes, increasing in several steps to 35% for incomes of $372,000 or above. Income taxes are not usually a serious burden to families. Of course we all object, but that is not surprising considering that a government is not an easy thing to identify as a purchased service. It is a service nonetheless. If you don't believe it, move to Iraq or Rwanda or Bangladesh.

Incomes have skyrocketed since our current tax code was first conceived. But tax rates have not moved to compensate. Annual incomes of $10 million to $200 million were not even on the horizon at the end of WWII. Although not common, they exist today. In all fairness, such incomes are primarily for show. No one can or does spend $10 or $30 million in a year. It would be extremely challenging to try. So instead of capping the tax rate at 35%, it should continue to increase on money that is performing nothing, either for this economy or the individual receiving it. I suggest that tax rates for the first $372,000 to $1 Million be taxed at rates of 37%. Incomes from $1 million to $10 million should be taxed at a rate of 40%. Incomes from $10 million to $100 million be taxed at 50%, and incomes above $100 million should be taxed at 60%. Such a policy would make corporate directors think twice about granting such outrageous salaries to executives. They would come up with better uses for that money and, hopefully, more creative ways to compensate their outstanding executives.

We have similar problems with the capital gains tax. That, too, is income and should be taxed as such. The original purpose of the capital gains tax was to encourage investment in higher risk new ideas and new ventures. Applied as it is today if your Exxon Mobil stock increases 50% in value, you get a special "Capital Gains" consideration in taxes. Why? Exxon Mobil didn't get that money. You and the previous stockowner got that money and the next owner will get the money when he sells. Why does that earn special tax consideration? If you do indeed invest in a new idea or a new company and the company actually gets the money, it is in the nation's interest to give special tax consideration to that investment to encourage such new ventures. Capital gains tax rates should apply only to funds that actually financed the new venture or idea. Today their original purpose has been almost completely lost.

We have complaints about double taxation because dividends were paid out of taxed income of the corporation. The proposed remedy would eliminate the tax on dividends received. That doesn't help the company or the country. If there is to be tax relief on dividends it should go to the company that paid those dividends. They no longer gain from money they paid out in dividends. Why tax a corporation on income it gives to stockholders? That might even stimulate more corporations to pay dividends, a practice often ignored today. The recipient, not the company, should be taxed on that income.

Our tax laws are off kilter because they are so complex that most legislators who vote on them cannot understand them. I would not be surprised if it were done that way on purpose. Don't set up a system that requires a candidate for office to be a CPA. We have better things to do than to burden our legislators with trivia. A greatly simplified pay-as-you-go tax code would bring sighs of relief from every facet of society, with the possible exception of those with incomes over $1 million per year. They are already spending that money on lobbyists trying to get additional tax breaks for those who need it least. Why not give a new, more equitable tax structure a try?

CHAPTER 24
Terrorism—Our Lost Focus

We have lost our direction. The world is threatened by a violently resurgent plague of misplaced religious militarism. Our problem is the way we think. As a nation, we tend to deal with other nations, but this has little if anything to do with nations. This insurgency has been growing for over twenty-five years and still we tend to talk of it in term of the nations in which it is now prevalent. We speak of Afghanistan, Iraq, Iran, Saudi Arabia and Turkey and Syria, but none of these countries is the source of the problem. They may be invaded by the movement, but they are not the source.

When we attacked Afghanistan, the dynamic started to move toward Iraq. When we attacked Iraq, it tended to move back to Afghanistan and elsewhere as well. We find it in Pakistan, Iran, and in Sudan. We find tiny enclaves in France, in Holland, in Spain.

The problem is our way of thinking. We think in terms of nationality, but this is cultural. It may be religious, but it primarily is tribal. We forget that this movement arises in an area of the world where tribes and minicultures have been dominant for millennia. While the outside world has moved toward nations and national agendas, that has only been superimposed on a part of the world where culture is much more closely confined. If you read the bible, you will find conflicts by the hundreds between small groups that were bigger or smaller because they happened to have, or not to have, a particularly charismatic leader.

The geographic lines changed frequently, but the cultural divides remained. Today, as with the Old Testament, these people, still believe in the clan and the tribe. Nationality is a secondary loyalty to them and often either changes or disappears altogether. In Iraq, it is more important that you are a Kurd, a Sunni or a Shiite, than that you are an Iraqi. A few people have grown out of that way of thinking, but the bulk of the locals have not. Even within these cults, small militias and warlords tend to dominate fractions of the culture, and the conflicts within them are almost as frequent as the conflicts between them.

This is not a military conflict. A roadside bomb is not a military weapon! It has no target. It kills anyone who comes along, friend and foe alike. This is a conflict of ideas, and these are not new ideas. They have been active for hundreds of years. Semi-successful trends to coalesce the many tribes into larger cultures under a particularly strong leader have had few successes and even fewer that lasted for very many generations. Even Mohammed, in creating Islam, had a short influence. With the death of his grandson in 687 the Mohammedan culture became divided against itself as Sunnis and Shiites found more fault with each other than they did with the rest of the world. They fought not only the infidel, but also each other. It continues to this day.

We need to look carefully at the internal workings of problems we face. As a country that believes in and thrives on nationalism, it is hard for us to look at the rest of the world in other terms. But that portion of the world does not really understand "nationality." We will not make any real progress in this war on terrorism until we can begin to address the world that we are facing——not nations, but tribes and clans and small cults.

One of the problems is that these subcultures are still, like 3000 years ago, dominated by petty egotistical leaders whose main objective is to gain control. One of the ways they do that is to keep followers ignorant. Most of the Islamic leaders oppose education, particularly for women. They have a huge supply of 12 to 25 year-olds who can neither read nor write, and have little understanding of, or interest in, other cultures. They are underemployed and deprived. But they have cell phones! As such they are a prey to violent solutions because they aren't educated enough to devise better ones. Their egotistical imams teach hatred successfully, because their followers have no ability to assess their "enemies." It is easy to convince a poor, unemployed 18 year-old that committing suicide and going to the Promised Land is better than trying to live in a scorched earth. The promise of seventy virgins is so obviously wrong, that even a small education can see through that. Sex is a fleshly pleasure. The one thing we know for certain that we do NOT take to the hereafter is flesh.

Until we western nationalists learn the nature of the culture we fight, we will struggle. We use their tools of violence and fight on their terms in their territory. We do not even approach the root causes of our conflict. We complain that their government does not accomplish its task, but they have no democratic background, no cultural concept of a nation and no experience in uniting clashing tribes. It is far better to employ and educate those hotheaded youths than to kill them, but we aren't even trying. We are relying upon their cultural leaders to teach the youth things that those leaders don't understand or believe in themselves. Where's the path to success in that?

Why don't we have massive propaganda programs which blanket the area with the truth and opportunity, much like Radio Free Europe in WWII? Stop talking about Iraq and Iran. Those countries were created 85 years ago by nationalistic outsiders. Their purpose was to prevent the resurgence of the Ottoman Empire. Outsiders lumped together warring cults and tribes that have been in conflict ever since. Talk about the real culprits——Shiites, Sunnis, Kurds and militias. Negotiate with the imams and clerics, and let them divide their territories according to local custom instead of western national boundaries. Bring education, not weapons. Bring employment, and divert that source of gullible youth. Stop buying their oil, which finances the very petty tyrants we want to overcome. We will not win by destroying. We will win by teaching! As Barack Obama said recently, we will be remembered by what we build, not by what we destroy.

The militant activists claim that their opponents want to cut and run. NO WAY! As we remove soldiers, replace them with sensitive, knowledgeable people who want to bring old warring factions together, stop the senseless killing and create a better future for those who now believe that the world is so bad that only violence can save it. What they need instead of funerals is hope. The truth will set them free. It may set us all free!

We have an enormous opportunity. The world is in the largest transformation of communication in all history. The Internet will have a much larger impact on society than the printing press or even the radio. It already has! Cell phones are everywhere, and, like most new things, are being abused more than they are being used. It is used by the greedy to persuade the ignorant and the uneducated. Let's take a page from their book and spread knowledge and information. Teach cooperation, not conflict. Television, radio, the Internet, cell phones. These are the weapons of this war. We are lagging behind in their use. We do so at our peril, and at the peril of the entire world.

CHAPTER 25
Sub-Prime Mortgages-A Rip-off

The sub-prime mortgage was an ill-conceived expansion of the usurious "interest only" mortgage. It was yet another scheme to entice unqualified homebuyers into homes they couldn't afford. Its only purpose was to increase home sales. Banks and mortgage lenders have already stacked the cards in their own favor for over 100 years. Why else would they charge the poor, who had to struggle, a higher interest rate than to the rich, who didn't need help? The idea that loans should be tailored to the needs of the bank instead of the borrower is a bad idea. Extending it to the working poor was merely a scheme to expand an already lucrative market. It should have been stopped at its inception.

But bad as that is, the response to the crisis is even worse. We bail out the perpetrator, not his victim. This outrage is excused by the accusation that the real problem was the many people who bought several homes during an explosive valuation increase, so that they could rent them out and reap the benefits of market appreciation. Many of those were interest only mortgages, so that the buyer/speculator could minimize his payments and maximize his rental income. Since housing prices were growing at an unprecedented rate he could cash in any time by selling the house for more than he paid for it. Of course many opportunists did buy several homes, but that has an easy fix.

If the Fed would force the lender to perpetuate the initial payment scheme for the life of the mortgage, the poor buyer would be able to keep his home. But limit that freeze to the first-time owner who lives in the house. The speculator should not have that option. Neither should it apply to interest only mortgages, which should be banned altogether.

Let's look at the interest only mortgage. Who ever dreamed up such an obvious scam to get someone permanently into your debt? It surely wasn't the homebuyer. It should never have been allowed in the first place and it should be outlawed immediately. Why does our Fed allow bankers and lenders to prey upon the poor family man who is hardly competent to understand high finance and shouldn't be required to? He is vulnerable, and easily misled. The problem is that the home being financed is touted as the perfect home, when a less expensive home is not only adequate, but probably could serve his needs better. The complicit real estate agent often portrays this as the perfect home, when his data sheets show that is too costly for that buyer. The agent has no data showing that the buyer will have an increase in income to meet the increased payment when the initial stage is completed. But the risk, in a time of increasing valuation, applies not to the banker, who can foreclose, but the homeowner who can't make the increased payment. Putting thousands of people in homes that were more than they could afford is a con game and the whole country is suffering because a few bankers wanted to get rich. Bankers and real estate agents have pages of charts and formulas, which identify the size of a mortgage that can be supported by a given level of income. The buyer has no such data. But with an interest only, or a sub-prime mortgage, they squeezed the buyer. If he can't pay, the banker can foreclose and resell the property for a higher price. The banker gets protected at the expense of the buyer. The buyer gets thrown out on the street.

The banker was already protected. He charged a higher interest rate because the struggling buyer is a risky borrower according to banker logic. Every facet of this whole plan is designed to protect the banker, not the borrower. The borrower is the tool, and the borrower became the victim.

Mohammed Yunus has proved to the world with his Grameen Bank, that the working poor are better at paying back loans than the rich folk. Maybe the banking industry doesn't want to learn from that experience, but it should. A strong work ethic is a better indicator of the sense of responsibility than money in the bank. That comes as no surprise to most of us who have to work for a living. Why does it shock bankers? Isn't that their business? Now the whole country is being squeezed because of their ill-conceived idea. Since their scheme has backfired with a declining housing market, the bankers and moneylenders should bear that burden themselves. Their sub-prime, interest only and adjustable rate mortgage (ARM) were major factors in both the market increase and the subsequent market decline. They had already reaped great undeserved rewards from that market. Now, homeowners are carrying that burden instead of the moneylender. This is not new. Christ threw the moneylenders out of the temple. Why don't we? Instead of a golden parachute, send them to jail for fraud! Their long-standing "greedy" reputation looks well deserved today.

CHAPTER 26
Who's in There?

I was concerned about the issues of the race for party nominees for president. This nation is facing enormous problems—monumental problems. We face global warming with an apathetic population that doesn't know how to attack the problem. We face a worldwide threat from people who want to destroy lifestyles and governments by any means including violence. We face an economic crisis in which that mass of people who built this as a strong nation is becoming disenfranchised and shoved aside. But the issues that seem to dominate the political agenda most are race and gender. Why?

I am white. I am not white by choice. It just happened that way. Barack Obama is black or at least half black. He didn't choose to be that way. That's the package in which he was delivered. Hillary Clinton is female. She didn't choose to be female—that's the way she came. Being black or female doesn't make either of them better or worse people. It's what's inside that makes them who they are. What do they do? What do they believe? Where are they going? Have they demonstrated the ability to accomplish their goals? That's what elections are all about. That's what makes an elected official either good or bad or just another politician.

The challenge to voters is to strip away all that visible, but insignificant exterior and find out who's in there. Sure, being black automatically presents a specific set of experiences. So too, being female. But what's important is what they did with that experience. What will they do to make it work for us all? Because when they get elected, they work for us all.

The press is not very good at stripping away the packaging and finding out what's in it. That's your job. Dig in. Find out. Look and evaluate. Of course you are dealing with the future—the great unknown. Futures grow out of pasts. You have the ability to hedge your bets on that future. Take the time to do it right. That may require you to strip away some of your own prejudices and get to the core of the election process. Who can lead us all in the right direction for a better country? Or, perhaps a better world, because we are a global world? We must think beyond our borders. Our children will compete with people from China, India, Australia, Europe and The Union of SouthAfrica. Who can help them be ready for that? And most important of all—how?

CHAPTER 27
Recession

There is talk of entering a recession. We already have one! Job growth is down, unemployment is up and income is down. We just set a new record in housing foreclosures, and had a major increase in job losses. How else would you define recession? It is generally accepted academically that a recession is defined as two consecutive quarters of declining Gross National Product. The problem is that by that time the damage is already done. People are hurting and worried. What can we do about that?

I don't know about other recessions, but this one is not necessary. We are sitting on one of the greatest opportunities of a century— alternate energy. The world needs alternate energy desperately and we have the science to accomplish it. Science, yes, but technology no! We have been studying alternate sources of energy for a century, but have brought very little of what we have learned to practical usage.

It is something of a mystery as to why. The need is obvious. We have watched the price of oil, our major energy source quintuple in seven years, but we haven't seen anywhere near that increase in solar, wind, geothermal, hydrogen or other alternatives. Is that because we don't know how? No! It is because it is easier just to pump more oil. However, oil is a limited resource, and is largely in the control of antagonistic regimes. Despite this, our government subsidizes over \$4 billion annually to the most profitable industry in our economy——oil! This allows that industry to pay \$147/barrel for oil, which it resells at an enormous profit, while Joe Workingman can't afford to fill his gas tank.

Do you see a connection here? Suppose we stopped the $4 billion subsidy to the oil industry and subsidized instead small, new alternate energy companies. How many jobs would that create? Unemployment would go down, and thousands of new jobs would be created every month.

It is easy to find fault, but finding solutions is much more difficult. We are officially in a war. That war directly affects less than 1% of our nations people. Our idea of patriotism is to paste a ribbon on the back of our car. Why don't we introduce gas rationing? Then the war would become part of everyone's life, and we could easily see the need for action. The auto industry, which says it can't develop 50-mpg vehicles for another ten years, would have one next year—count on it! In addition, we should by law decrease our total oil imports by 1% every month, and use the money saved to further support clean alternate energy. We should selectively reduce purchases from nations that support terrorists, which includes Saudi Arabia. Our oil purchases are supporting terrorists.

Would this be a perfect solution? No! We will make mistakes, and frauds will assuredly occur. Mistakes are how we learn. They will be sorted out quite quickly as we reorient our society to a host of alternatives to oil. The cheaters will be found, and the gougers will be marginalized. It will take a little while, but not 30 years! And the price of gasoline will go down almost immediately.

Gas rationing in WWII was remarkably effective. It was not much favored by anyone, but we all supported it. It was a little painful, but less painful than the alternative. It will be painful again, but if carefully explained will gain public support. It will not gain the support of the oil industry, however, and they will lobby against it. But who's in charge here, the oil industry, or the citizens? Right now the oil industry is, but I don't see why this nation should support paying $180 million/year to the president of Exxon, which has reported the largest profits of any company in the history of this country for each of the last three quarters, while I can't afford to fill my gas tank. Do you?

CHAPTER 28
Farewell Elliot Spitzer

The resignation of Elliot Spitzer as Governor of New York is a sad commentary on American politics. It is yet another incidence of the loss of a good elected official because of a personal failing which did not really affect his job performance. It is sad because, at the time of his resignation, we did not really know what, if any, crime he had committed. He didn't admit to anything specific and there was neither indictment nor trial. I thought, in America, that a person was innocent until proven guilty. Not if you're a politician.

Americans live in a dream world. They expect their public officials to be flawless people who have never made any mistakes. They don't expect the same from themselves. I've not only never met such a person, I've never even heard of a real one. Am I saying that what Elliot Spitzer is accused of doing is OK? No way! But what I am saying is that it is not an official duty of the Governor of New York, which duties he appears to have carried out diligently and accurately. In fact, that is why he was targeted in the first place. Who has more reason to wire tap an elected official than someone who has been hurt by his actions? And, indeed, Elliot Spitzer was not gentle or forgiving in his actions. It appears that the easiest way to shoot down a politician is to find some sexual misbehavior. That has been going on at least since King David, and David has a long line of successors. Human nature, being what it is, is not likely to go away in a big hurry. Man is a sexual being, which may explain why we have 7 billion people on an earth that may not be able to sustain 5 billion long term.

So New York should mourn the fall of Elliott Spitzer. He was a good governor and did many good things for that state. He very likely could have done much more. He has to do a lot of explaining to his wife and daughters, but not much to the State of New York and its people. It is the press that has crucified him, not his wife and daughters.

So, for the future, we would all be well to separate personal problems from problems on the job. Don't expect perfect people in our public life. There aren't any! Mark my words. We will find flaws in our latest messiah, Barack Obama, before his term is complete. We have been ever increasing our invasion of the privacy of our public officials. We, and the press, should ask if he doing a good job. If he is, those extracurricular activities should not disqualify him. We don't have to like him, but we do have to like the job he is doing.

CHAPTER 29
Energy Independence

President Bush said in his 2006 State of the Union speech that we are addicted to oil. In fact, we are addicted to energy consumption, and oil is the cheapest and easiest source of energy—today! But that era is coming to a close. Oil is getting scarcer, harder to extract and more difficult to process. The price goes up and will continue to go up.

But our government has taken no positive steps to minimize our dependence or to seek alternative sources of energy. In fact, it continues to provide grants and subsidies to our most profitable industry.

Many of us seem to think that some brilliant solution will appear like sunrise to solve the problem. In reality, however, there will not be one, but many solutions. This is a highly desirable outcome, because it moves control of energy sources from a few big monopolies to a diverse group of competitive suppliers. When the price of gasoline goes up today, you have no choice but to pay it. If there were many alternatives, you could opt for another source.

We are faced with two energy problems, which, although related, are not the same. The first is that we are dependent upon sources of oil from unstable foreign governments that would like to manipulate the price and supply not only to squeeze as much money as possible out of this wealthy nation, but also for political purposes. Oil is and will increasingly become a political tool. Venezuela, Saudi Arabia, Iran and Russia already wield this power ruthlessly. It will get worse. That is why we are in Iraq.

The second problem is that our two largest energy sources are serious greenhouse gas emitters. We are creating global warming that is already beginning to cause serious long-term problems not only in the United States, but to the whole world. When we seek solutions, we need to face both of these problems, but not necessarily with the same urgency. Ultimately we must develop renewable energy to cease or greatly reduce greenhouse gas emissions. We must keep both problems in mind as we seek solutions.

Those are not the only reasons. Fossil fuels are a finite resource and we will eventually run out. Many people don't want to believe that, but finite is finite. We are attacking that supply with ever-increasing vigor. We already are surprised at how much we have drained that resource. The truth is that we have less than we claim we do. Oil reserves in Saudi Arabia, Iraq and Iran are seriously overstated. The question is not if we will run out of such sources, but when?

The ultimate solution to the greenhouse gas emissions is in its source. Eventually fossil fuels will run out. Without some serious effort from mankind, that will not occur until we have already put all that carbon back into our atmosphere and our oceans and made our planet as warm and as lifeless as Venus.

Oil is our dominant source of energy because it is the most adaptable, cost-efficient and available source. There can be no single replacement for oil. There will be hundreds, each adapted for a particular niche, or set of niches. If they are to be long-term solutions, they must be renewable—-which ultimately means solar, tidal or geothermal. There is an abundance of solar energy. It comes in many forms, none of which is extensively utilized today. Wind and waterfalls are two major underutilized sources of solar energy. Solar heating and photovoltaics are also grossly underutilized. As the price of oil continues to rise each of these will become ever more economically viable sources.

Windmills powered the farms of the Midwest and the west for over 100 years. Solar panels have been around for over fifty years. There is a small resurgence of these alternatives but they will not become practical unless and until we all push to make it happen. Big businesses, those who now hold the purse strings to energy, oppose such developments. Alternative sources would wrest control of energy from them. We already suffer from over-centralization of energy sources. When electric power costs double, we pay it because we have no choice. How do you battle the only supplier of a critical resource? Since those commercial interests lobby our government, and form political action committees (PAC's) to elect favorable government officials, government is unwilling to wrest control from them and put it in the hands of the people who, ultimately, pay for it. It will take a massive effort by <u>all</u> of us to bring about the changes we need for our future energy needs. What can you do to regain energy independence? It is not enough to complain and to point fingers or even write your congressman—it is essential that each of us does something every day if we really want to solve the energy problems we face.

Probably the largest and easiest part of the solution is to reduce our energy demands. This approach addresses both the global warming issue and the single source issue. Our automotive industry builds 360 horsepower engines, driving massive vehicles at outrageous speeds. They want you to build a home on four wheels and drive it from 0 to 60 in 4 seconds. What for? Where? 260 of those horsepower are completely unnecessary. Equating bigger with better is an American quirk. The auto industry says that they are building the cars that Americans want, but have you seen their ads? Which of you wants to put your car into a 360° skid in a wet school parking lot, or drive along a cliff at the edge of Grand Canyon? Those ads are aimed at the 22 year-old macho male who can't afford such a car anyhow. The luxury things in a large car can easily be put in a small car. They already do that in Europe. Luxury cars should be the Jewel, the Diamond, the Gem or the Sapphire—small but extremely high quality. The Hummer and the Escalade should disappear. They are the epitome of wastefulness. These ego-driven examples of conspicuous consumption are detrimental to society and to the future.

How does one achieve this change? Much of it is re-education of our public. This is such a massive problem that it will take all of us to conquer it. What have <u>you</u> done to solve these problems?

Some of it can be guided by national tax policy. For example, the tax rate on vehicles should increase as their emissions increase. Germany and some American states already have attempted to impose an emissions tax. It might be easier to enact a horsepower tax—$50 on every additional horsepower above 100 in a new vehicle. That would put a $13,000 tax on a 360 HP Infinity. Even if that 360 HP is modified to run on hydrogen, it still places a huge and unnecessary energy demand that will strain our energy sources. Such a vehicle could escape the pollution tax, but not the horsepower tax. The customer still has a choice. It is up to him to decide. That tax money should be reserved for developing alternate sources of energy.

Another source, destroyed by a coalition of auto, rubber and oil companies in the early 1930's, is public transportation. That requires a slow rebuilding process and lots of capital, but it has public support. The MTA, Boston's subway system, had the largest ridership in its history in 2008.

Then, there's the bicycle. Short intra-urban trips could easily be made on a bicycle, which is non-polluting, and might help solve our national obesity problem. People could demand the addition of bicycle lanes on our city streets, and may even ask for tax relief for the miles they don't drive.

Alternative sources of energy must ultimately rely on less limited supplies of energy: the sun, the tides, ocean currents, wind, waterfalls, the oceanic thermocline and geothermal energy. The faster we raid all our sources of stored energy, the more we hasten the arrival of a day of reckoning.

The immediate problem is oil. We increasingly demand oil from areas in the world with unstable governments. The probability that some despot will come to power and try to hijack oil supplies for his own purposes is high and increasing. King Abdullah, our supposed ally, is already doing just that. Coal, a temporary solution to the oil dilemma, is more abundant than oil, but is more difficult to use. It is also in abundance right here in the United States, as was oil 100 years ago. Coal is a more serious pollution threat. Coal has a larger percentage of carbon than oil, so it emits more greenhouse gases. It also contains more pollutants like sulfur, arsenic and mercury. Since it tends to burn hotter than oil, it produces more nitrogen oxides. But the technology to minimize those emissions has been known for over 80 years. A few companies have employed these techniques but most go the easier route. They use oil.

Coal, like oil, is a finite resource—-it can and will be depleted. Coal cannot be used everywhere. Your hot water heater, your stove, your automobile and your clothes drier would be extremely difficult and expensive to convert to coal. There are other choices. Many appliances are already electric powered—a wasteful and inefficient response. Many of us think that an electric stove is non-polluting, but the fact is that it is more so, but the pollution occurs at the power station instead of at your house. Why not convert gas stoves, driers and hot water heaters to hydrogen? That can be a completely non-polluting fuel that could be used in any of those appliances with a minor change costing less that $20. Automobiles can run on hydrogen. This, too, would take some of the monopolistic control of energy from the few massive oil companies to many independent suppliers from more diverse sources.

Hydrogen is very difficult to store. It takes up lots of space. To use it in transportation is difficult at best because you must carry a large container with you. But, somehow, transportation has absorbed most of the effort on hydrogen because it would replace our largest single consumer of oil.

Hydrogen can be manufactured by wind and/or solar-powered electrolysis of ocean water. It can be generated by power from ocean currents, which contain about 100 times as much energy as wind. The mass of the earth's oceans is 300 times the mass of the earth's atmosphere. Water is 1000 times as dense as air and can drive turbines more effectively. In addition, ocean currents flow steadily all the time, unlike the winds. Still further, if we create water driven power equipment for the ocean currents, it can also be used in our rivers and streams. Most of our nation is over 200 miles from an ocean current, but almost everyone lives within 100 miles of a river and within 10 miles of a stream. Wind and water are truly unlimited resources capitalizing on an available but underused source of energy—the sun!

Strictly speaking, hydrogen is not a source of energy because it is not naturally occurring. It must be man-made. It is a superb medium for the transport and delivery of energy. Currently, hydrogen is made commercially in the U.S. by nine different industrial processes. The largest of those is from methane—a carbon based gas. Producing hydrogen from methane merely transfers the source of pollution from the user to the manufacturer, and it still depletes our natural energy reserves. Where's the long-term gain? Only one of those nine sources doesn't require fossil fuels—hydrolysis of water. (The reaction of steam on iron and the dissociation of ammonia are not direct contributors to greenhouse gases, but each requires high temperatures that need either fossil fuels or electricity to achieve.) Hydrolysis is currently the smallest source of commercial hydrogen. But when made from renewable sources we progress toward independence from oil and finite stored energy sources, and reduce global warming at the same time. Wind farms producing electrolytic hydrogen instead of electricity could help close the gap. In addition it would be another step toward escaping the monopoly of "The Grid." In addition, they should be out to sea where they do not cause NIMBY complaints from neighbors and land need not be fought over and purchased. The wind there is steadier and blows much closer to the sea surface than it does over vegetated land. Your towers need not be so high. In fact several levels can be stacked on each platform. The problem of wires and cables would be eliminated as well as the difficulty in phasing to the alternating current of the power grid. Best of all, it will disperse rather than concentrate the sources of power. No more monopolies. No more Enrons! A wind and/or ocean current driven hydrolysis station at sea would cost less than an oil-drilling rig.

To carry us through the transition period we could go to the oil sands of Canada and the shale oils of Colorado and the Rocky Mountains. These oil sources are more difficult to extract, but there is a huge supply of them and they are out of OPEC control. They could produce an enormous cash flow for Canada, and reduce our dependence upon oil from politically unstable governments. The technology already is in commercial use. Oil sands are far more effective than drilling in the Alaska National Wildlife Refuge and less expensive. They are more expensive than oil or coal, but with the recent increases in oil prices are becoming more nearly cost competitive. Oil sands and oil shales will <u>not</u> solve the greenhouse gas problem. Nor will they break big oil's stranglehold on energy sources, since big oil and coal interests already own much of the oil shale and oil sands. Beware! Like almost every mining process and other methods of using environmental sources, the oil sands industry is creating in Alberta a massive wasteland out of what was once a primeval forest. Man has a history if destroying nature in order to gain its benefits. We have the opportunity to stop this destruction, but we haven't even tried so far. We are creating a wasteland larger than Manhattan in Alberta—unnecessarily!

Electricity is already supplied largely through coal. Although some power plants are reasonably good at controlling pollution, they all could and should be far more so. The technology and equipment to do so has been available for 50 years. Greed and concern for the next quarter's bottom line have delayed their introduction. The coal industry has been touting "sequestering" of the carbon dioxide emissions for over 15 years but they have yet to build the first such plant.

But there is another option—nuclear. That is a frightening concept for most of us—primarily because of Chernobyl, Three Mile Island and ignorance. Nuclear energy can be made safe. It already is.

America's big disaster in nuclear energy at Three Mile Island injured no one, although it frightened millions of people. It occurred because there were three levels of management failure. Three Mile Island got out of hand because of inadequate training and preparation for a failure. Even with Chernobyl, nuclear power has a far better safety record than coal. It would be far less polluting to the atmosphere.

Nuclear waste is a soluble problem. We haven't done much yet. There are two kinds of nuclear waste—-High-level waste with a half-life of more than 100 years, and low level waste with a half-life of 100 years or less. (A half-life is the time it takes a radioactive material to radiate away half of its radioactive mass). Much of the high level waste can be reprocessed and made into fuel rods for nuclear power plants. Think about this. Nuclear materials existed on earth before we mined them, concentrated them and refined them. We can dilute the low level waste and return it to the mines where their precursors came from as part of a mine reclamation plan. We restore the mines, produce no more hazards than we started with, and shorten the time of exposure by 99%. In addition, the reclamation should include the planting of trees, the major land-based atmospheric cleaning agent.

There is another advantage to the use of nuclear power. Think about this. What can be concentrated can also be diluted. Why not dilute weapons grade nuclear materials of which there is a great abundance, to fuel grade nuclear materials? (This is already being done on a small scale.) Such a move would gradually deplete the supply of extremely risky weapons grade materials, which are subject to compromise by egotistical despots. It would also provide power for an increasingly demanding human race. We could ban uranium mining until the subsidized dilution of weapons grade materials has consumed all the nuclear weapons. By then the growth of other alternate energy sources should make further mining of uranium unnecessary. We all need fuel, but none of us needs nuclear bombs.

Gasoline is an extremely volatile and hazardous material. Despite that, we have learned to handle it safely. This country probably doesn't have half-a-dozen serious accidents a year in the transfer of gasoline to automobiles. Nuclear fuels should be able to have an even better record at least partly because it will only go to major nuclear installations. No one will have a nuclear furnace in his home, or a nuclear powered automobile. But nuclear energy, like oil and coal, is a finite reserve. Large, yes, but finite nonetheless. It is valuable primarily as a stopgap measure and as an anti terrorist measure. It emits no greenhouse gases.

Solar power is an underutilized resource mostly because it is intermittent, inefficient and unreliable. Most of us have a small solar powered hand calculator. Solar powered hot water systems and electric generators exist, but are expensive and unreliable. We extract only a small percentage of solar energy with most of our solar devices. Nonetheless, whole homes are powered by solar energy. That is just one more example that shows that the ultimate source of our energy is primarily sunlight. It is plentiful and universally available on an intermittent basis. We have developed some remarkably sophisticated solar energy systems that remain largely unused. The sun provides more energy every day than all mankind uses. We have learned to capture an insignificant amount for practical use. We are still learning and have much new science that has yet to be converted to technology.

Wind power is just one facet of solar power. It is the uneven heating of the earth by sunlight that causes wind. As long as the sun shines, wind power will be available.

So far most wind power has been operated by major power plants. In California there is a huge wind farm of over 600 windmills. Much of Western Europe, like Norway, Denmark, England and Holland use wind power. The problem with our present system is that it puts more electricity onto a grid that is controlled by a small number of commercial ventures. A major objective of energy policy should be to wrest much of that control from monopolistic mega companies and move it to smaller enterprises or individuals. Do you believe that gasoline would cost four dollars per gallon if there were 200 competing oil companies instead of seven? If a substantial portion of our home energy consumption came from individual wind generators, massive blackouts would be far less of a problem. Make no mistake, our electric power companies have been remarkably responsive to public need and to uninterrupted power flow. However, they are motivated primarily by the economics of the bottom line. Remember Enron? Remember the California energy crunch of 2003? In addition, having substantial supplies off the grid would ease the problems in times of blackouts from major snowstorms, earthquakes, floods or hurricanes.

Wind has its problems. It is unpredictable and extremely variable. In addition, our use of wind has been dominated by industry. They want to build huge windmills and make big wind farms to feed energy onto the grid so that they retain control. But the big windmills, although efficient when they are operating, won't operate in winds below 8MPH—a condition that occurs less than 30% of the time in most of the U.S. One cure for that is to design them to work at only 4 or 3 mph. That will essentially triple the operating time of a wind generator. Perhaps such a windmill will be less efficient when operating, but will operate three times as much. In addition, windmills should be at sea where the wind blows stronger, closer to the surface and much more steadily. At sea you won't have to buy land and the towers need not be so tall or so expensive.

Still better, we should create an industry of building small windmills (400 to 1500 watts) that work on your rooftop. The complaint is that they make too much noise, but that is a soluble problem. You need not go to the grid for power and when a major power outage occurs, you will still be operating.

Tides are a little-used source of energy. Near coastlines tide derived power could add to the complex mixture of energy sources. Much of the world's shoreline has breakwaters to control the erosion and impact of tides. Why don't we insert hundreds of small water generators in these breakwaters? They will generate electricity as the tide comes in and generate more when the tide goes out.

Waterfalls, like Niagara Falls, are other sources of solar power. We have also used dams like Boulder Dam, and Grand Coulee Dam, but they have other environmental impacts that make them less viable. We are, finally, learning to cope with those problems. Opening the gates periodically, simulating the spring floods, has already made considerable restoration of the downstream environment on the Colorado River.

Geothermal energy is another useable source of energy. All of Iceland's electricity is generated by geothermal energy. It can be done elsewhere as well. Although sparsely distributed over the earth, geothermal areas are waiting for development in many parts of the world. No, it is not desirable to cap Old Faithful for geothermal energy. Geothermal energy is everywhere. Almost anywhere in the world we can dig small geothermal wells and provide some of the heat required to heat a home. They also have the advantage of offering cooling in the summer. We need more of that.

Energy abounds. We have capitalized on almost none of it, because oil was easier. Oil's heyday has been. It is time we looked seriously at alternatives that have been touted for decades, but remain largely undeveloped because oil was too cheap. The subsidies and tax breaks won by the oil industry should be redirected toward development of alternative energy. When we have an oil crisis, like the political instability of the OPEC nations, of course the oil industry wants permission to drill in The Alaska National Wildlife Refuge. That will increase their dominant control of our energy supply. But take a look at Prudhoe Bay. That environmental disaster is what our wildlife refuge will look like, not just for ten years, but forever. We have left the development of alternative energy sources to commercial enterprises. To increase the bottom line, they have taken the oil route. It is time for that government, which supposedly is more interested in the long term welfare of the nation than today's bottom line, to divert the huge tax beaks from the world's most profitable companies to the start-up companies of the future. Oil's days are numbered and we must wake up to that fact before a crisis arrives. That may not be that far in the future with China and

India, coming into that market. If 20% of our energy came from oil, rather than 80%, we would have no crisis today. We have used more oil than we have discovered for over thirty years now, and that is why the battle for energy gets so intense. It is highly likely that the calculated oil reserves in Arabia and the Mideast are grossly overstated. That means that the oil crisis is more imminent than we want to admit. So why delay finding alternatives? So far it is merely to preserve fat bottom lines for our current energy suppliers—at the expense of the consuming public. It is worthy of note that as the price of a barrel of crude oil increases so do the profits of the oil companies. Where is their incentive to keep the price of oil down?

We must be careful in our search for alternative sources of energy to move toward truly unlimited sources like sun, wind, ocean currents, geothermal or tides. The use of coal, oil sands, natural gas and nuclear fuels are all good alternatives, but they are also finite and will become depleted. Biodiesel is another viable alternative, but recognize that there just isn't enough of it. At the very best we can expect it to supply about 8% of the diesel market. The same is true of corn-derived alcohol. There just isn't enough corn. But worse, is the problem that taking a product, like corn, from the food market, and using it in another causes major economic disruption. The price of beef has gone up substantially, and so has bread, as we convert acreage from wheat to corn to make government-subsidized ethanol. In addition, biodiesel and alcohol produce more CO2 per unit of energy than oil. And ethanol is a far worse greenhouse gas emitter than gasoline, because it is made by fermentation, which produces as much CO2 as it does alcohol even before you put in your gas tank. We should not subsidize ethanol, because there are far better ways of attacking the energy problem.

In summary, remember two major principles. There will not be a single replacement for oil as our primary source of energy— there will be many. As we move toward new sources, focus primarily on infinite sources such as sunlight, tides, geothermal or wind. Finite resources like oil shale, oil sands or even nuclear are valuable resources, but merely buy us the time to develop more efficient access to unlimited resources of energy. The sun supplies more energy to the earth than our current energy demand. But, to date, we only use a tiny fraction of that abundance. That is very disturbing, because the science to capitalize on most of those resources has been known for 100 years or more.

These are a few of hundreds of solutions to small parts of our oil dependence. There are already many more and the field is ripe for still others. If every one of us in this nation focuses on getting the job done piece by piece, we probably could cut our oil demand by half within five years. Why not? But it will take all of us. In addition, there are other benefits. Creating new sources of energy will also create jobs. For example we have many new technologies that are in the earliest stages of development. Why can't we take some of those to China and help them grow their economy without demanding more oil and coal, but by using our new and developing technologies. That will greatly boost our relationship with the largest nation on earth and will generate much international commerce to help reduce our outrageous international trade deficit.

In making these moves in the energy supply we have failed so far to distinguish between escaping dependence on oil from unstable countries and reducing greenhouse gas production. We have also ignored the fact that these finite resources will eventually be used up. These are all critical issues, but they are not the same issue. Some few moves can relieve all of these problems. However, that does not invalidate the use of others for specific purposes. Some of them may even be short term, but still contribute to the overall progress toward energy independence.

To reduce global warming, we have focused primarily upon cutting back emissions, but we have neglected the other half of the equation. How do we get rid of the greenhouse gases that already exist? Atmospheric CO_2 has increased from 280 ppm to 385 ppm just in the last 100 years. Man has added 4.12 billion tons of CO_2 to our atmosphere in the last 100 years. That is the highest it has been in at least 100,000 years.

The world's major air cleaner is the tree. Trees absorb CO2 from the air. Seaweed and algae do the same in the oceans and streams, but not nearly as much as trees on land. The trees of the United States contain more carbon than all the CO2 in the earth's atmosphere. Why don't we establish a requirement that every school child plants one tree every year she is in school? That will be 50 million trees a year—-about as many as they are cutting down in the Amazon Jungle in Brazil. But it is bigger than that. The oceans have absorbed four times as much man-made CO2 (16.5 billion tons) as our atmosphere. CO2 forms an acid in water, as any soda pop lover will tell you. We are gradually converting our oceans into a giant pool of soda pop, and we are destroying much marine life in doing so. Oysters and clams have problems making their shells and corals can't generate their skeletons as easily in an acid ocean. As we take CO2 out of the air, the CO2 in the ocean will return to the air where it came from, and make our reduction process much slower, but much more beneficial.

The main point of all this alternate energy is that we all need to do something. It is not enough to let government and big business do it. For example, if we were to introduce gas rationing along with reducing our national oil imports by1% per month, the alternate energy business would explode. Think of the jobs that just that one move would create. Unemployment would drop almost overnight. What would it do for our recession if the money we saved on imported oil were spent primarily on alternate energy? What would that do for the financing of Islamic terrorists in Arabia?

So far, we have not formulated a plan for reducing global warming or reducing dependence upon foreign oil. We talk a lot. We do little. Most of us think that it is the job of government and industry to solve our energy problem. It is ours. We don't even have a goal! For example: Set two goals: 1. Pick a year, like 2012, when we show a decrease in total greenhouse gas emissions. 2. Pick another year, like 2020 when we see a decrease in global CO2 from 385 ppm to 350. Then we know that we are on our way to the final goal—-280 ppm.

One final note. Not all of our oil problems come from politics or technology. If we continue to expand world population at 3-4% each year, there will come a time when no available resource or technology will be able to meet that energy demand, let alone our food demand. Are we prepared for that?

CHAPTER 30
English In America

The establishment of English as the official language in the United States would be a serious error, which defeats many of the benefits of our diverse society. On the other hand, non-English education is an equally serious mistake, which should be eliminated. Our people and our Congress seem to have a problem separating the functional need for a common language from the support of a diverse cultural heritage. I favor both.

Non-English education of some of our young automatically creates a second-class status for those students by denying them access to the main stream of our primarily English speaking country. We have enough barriers to interaction in American society. Let's not introduce language as another. Every member of our society should have some common language with which to communicate with fellow citizens. Since English is overwhelmingly predominant in American social intercourse, English should be that language if only for practical reasons. All public supported education in this country should be conducted in English. If it is, everyone will be able to speak to everyone else.

The establishment of English as the "Official" language of this country would tend to denigrate the value of other languages. English is not chosen because it is better than other languages. It isn't. It is chosen because it is the most common. The presence of other languages and other cultural heritages in the United States is precisely the strength that allows us to compete so favorably in the world. It is one source of the vigor of our nation. I strongly support the right or perhaps the need to have Americans speak as many other languages as possible and to experience as many cultures as possible. It is this diversity that allows us to understand and draw upon the myriad cultural strengths of this earth. In the 19th century we destroyed over 100 unwritten American Indian languages and the cultures they represented. We will sorely miss them for many centuries to come in our increasingly racist society. They could greatly enhance our ability to cope with the diverse cultural problems of this shrinking world.

To declare that non-English languages are inferior or unwanted in our land is both wrong and foolhardy. The establishment of an official language is an act of political dominance, not a move toward unity. We need a common language that brings us together, not an official language that keeps us apart.

The complaint about people speaking other languages is not facing the problem. It doesn't matter what language you speak in your home. That is a matter of personal choice. The problem arises when you can't speak English. Then you are cut off from a huge segment of our society. It is not important that you speak another language. What is important is that you must speak English to communicate with other Americans. If you can, all other language skills are assets. Let's not lose sight of the goal. We want a society in which every member can communicate with every other member. If we can, then we have reached a worthy goal.

CHAPTER 31
Social Security—The Mother of Retirement?

There is so much furor about social security today that it is almost impossible to figure out what the problem is let alone what the solution is. Partisans describe many views, and a variety of proposed solutions. There are extreme differences in the size and urgency of the problem, depending upon the viewpoint of the spokesman. Will it be broke in 2016 or 2055? Because of this wrangling, the public debate over the issue misses the most important facet of this complex subject. To gain an understanding of the whole issue, let's go back to the Great Depression when Social Security was introduced. There was 25% unemployment, and jobs were scarce. President Roosevelt recognized that many of those unemployed would end up on the public dole for the rest of their lives. No one had retirement income. If you were forced to quit, you had to rely on your savings—-many of which had been wiped out in the myriad bank failures.

A visionary Roosevelt, with the help of his cabinet and Congress, established the Social Security system, which benefited recipients as well as the federal government. If people paid into the system, that would relieve the demands upon the U.S. Treasury to support those who were unable to find employment. They established the "retirement" age for receiving benefits at 65—four years _older_ than the 61-year average life expectancy at birth in that year. There were 12 workers paying into the program for every beneficiary—soon going to 16 as employment rose.

This plan had some far-reaching side effects. Among them was establishing 65 as the age of "retirement". Industry adopted that concept with enthusiasm. There had been no "retirement" prior to 1932. Most workers couldn't work to age 65 because of illness, incapacitation or death. It provided employers a chance to retire people and move up the vigorous younger, but less experienced, employees.

One of the unintended consequences was felt about thirty years later. My father was in that first generation of people who actually lived long enough to "retire." And they did—in droves. They retired to do nothing but enjoy life. Life is not about doing nothing. Life exists for accomplishment. With no plans for this long awaited retirement, they literally bored themselves to death. I saw about a dozen of my father's close friends retire and die within nine, six or even three months. They had worked all their lives, and couldn't handle life without some difficult challenges.

In 2005 the life expectancy at birth was 77 years. And because of great advances in medicine and health, people are active and able well into their seventies. In addition, our society has become so much more complex that there are many jobs for which the prime requirement is experience—the very experience that 65 year-olds have in abundance. The laws say you can retire at 65, and industry reinforces it with policies drawn around that magic number.

Your elected representatives know that, but they don't mention it to you or anyone else. They are terrified of the consequences of raising the eligibility age. No congressman wants to increase the eligibility age for social security, because he thinks that the very mention of such a plan would vote him out of office.

Would it? What is so attractive about imposing a mandatory retirement upon active people who want to be productive and to feel needed? No one _needs_ a retiree who spends his days on the golf course—or worse yet stays home making life miserable for a spouse.

The life expectancy at birth of Americans has increased about 3 months every year for nearly 200 years. It shows no sign of slowing down. Today the eligibility for social security is 12 years younger than the life expectancy——a far cry from 1933. What do we get from all this? Today there are only four people working for every eligible retiree—one third of the 1933 ratio. That's why the payroll deductions kept rising for many years. It may get worse.

Look at another unintended consequence. We have a huge supply of active intelligent "retirees" who have many talents and want to use them. Vast numbers of retirees get bored and want to re-enter the work force. There are a few companies who make a point of hiring people over sixty-five. They are happy with the results. So are their employees, both young and old. Why abandon this valuable resource?

The fear of elected officials about increasing the age of eligibility is unfounded. Scaring the public by telling them that social security will be dead by the time they retire is not the solution. It certainly makes the raising of the eligibility age look like a better choice. Another government fear: "I paid that system for years and have nothing to show for it." Social Security is an insurance policy. It guarantees support when needed. It is not a get rich scheme. Do you ask for a refund of your auto insurance premium because you had no accidents last year? People aren't stupid. If they know the whole story, there will be a sigh of relief instead of an uproar. "There <u>will</u> be social security when I need it."

Different people get different numbers when calculating when social security goes broke, but the day will assuredly come if we fail to attack the real problem—demographics. We can change payment structures, privatize a portion of the payments, put it in a lock-box, increase the upper limit for payments or borrow the funds from other projects—all to no avail. The problem will not go away until we face the real threat—- people live longer, they are healthy longer, they are able to work longer and they want to. Eliminate the word "retirement" from our vocabulary. What we really want is "career change"—giving people an opportunity to accomplish something they always wanted to do, but couldn't afford to do. Get rid of that number 65, and attend to the true values and benefits of the system. Until we do, this debate will continue and get more heated. The solution that is in the best interests of all is staring us in the face, but we don't want to see it. Tie social security eligibility to the demographics of the health and ability of our citizens as it was in 1933.

It is easier to find fault than to find solutions. I propose:

First—Increase the age of eligibility for social security benefits by 5 months every year for 40 years. That way no one will be suddenly disenfranchised. Working people can easily calculate the age at which they can "change jobs" and receive social security support.

Second—Increase the upper income limit from which payroll deductions are taken out by $50,000 every year. Those who have gained most from our system need not get a bonus at the expense of others. This country provides opportunities. Those whose talents match those opportunities perfectly should gladly pay taxes to support that system without which they, too, might be paupers.

Third—Study and refine the means testing clause of social security. The very wealthy have already gained enormous benefit from our society. Don't bleed the public wealth by giving social security "perks" where they are not needed.

Fourth—Increase the disability allowances for those who become unable to work before they reach eligibility age. That's a safety net.

These four changes will make social security what it was meant to be and should remain—a security net for those too old or too disabled to work and for whom our bountiful society has not delivered the means to survive unemployed. It is even possible that somewhere along the way, the 6.2% payroll tax for social security (and Medicare) may be decreased!

People will love this idea, but industry probably will not. However, there is a way to satisfy both. At eligibility age, industry could give employees the option of working a 36-hour week or quitting and begin to draw any benefits for which they are eligible. That option remains each year except that the workweek decreases by two hours every year. At today's eligibility age of 65, qualified employees would work only 36 hours weekly. At age 66 it would lower to 34 hours. The workweek declines 2 hours per week each year after eligibility age. After eligibility age, as today, employees will have no social security deducted from their pay, and employers will no longer have to make matching payments. In eight years the workweek becomes 20 hours. Industry would then have a gradual plan for replacing its older workers while still capitalizing on their experience. This does not prevent an employer from terminating an employee who cannot work, or doesn't perform. In addition employees will have a plan to accomplish other things in their lives. That may include playing golf, or could be a new career.

CHAPTER 32
Exclusive!

The Mideast is in crisis. There is unrest at every level. The Palestinians and the Jews are at swords points, and don't seem to be approaching any sort of rapport. The Iraqi's oppose any outside interference, but are killing more of their own than they are of the "enemy." Religious belief is at the core of all this, but it shouldn't be. There is a way out. Religious clerics on all sides have it in their power to end it, but they aren't even trying. Many are joining and promoting the fray.

The situation in and around Israel spills over into every other Mideast conflict. It is true that the territory is the homeland of the Jews. Not for 57 years, but for 4,000 years. But it is also the homeland of the Arabs for 4,000 years or more. (It goes back to two Semitic ancestors——Isaac and Ishmael.) They have been occupying that territory together all that time. Not very peaceably, but co-existing. There is an issue that never comes up, however, which is the key to the whole problem. Each of their Gods (which in reality is one God interpreted differently by different people) sent a message to his people: "This is your homeland." But the message received was "This is not the homeland of anyone else." Neither God ever used the word "Exclusive." There is no reason that Jews and Palestinians can't live in the same land together just as Blue Jays and Grackles do. Why are Blue Jays and Grackles smarter than people? Perhaps it is because they focus on taking care of themselves instead of telling the others how they should behave.

A Jew can walk by a mosque on his way to the synagogue for prayer. A Palestinian can live peaceably next to an infidel whose private affairs cause him no harm. There is no need for exclusion. Exclusion is the source of conflict. The fear of being driven from home makes people do terrible things they would not otherwise consider. The problem with the west bank settlements was not that the Jews moved in—-it was that they tried to suppress or evict the Palestinians. The formation of the state of Israel in 1948 was an act of exclusion. It shouldn't have been. The very least that should have happened was the simultaneous formation of a Palestinian state—a problem the world has been trying unsuccessfully to resolve ever since. Even that would not have faced the real problem—Exclusion. The concept of the formation of a Jewish state was good—but to use it for the purpose of excluding Palestinians from their homeland was wrong. Jews have reached the Promised Land again—-but that is not enough. They want to throw everyone else out! They have been terrible neighbors. They are belligerent and confiscatory. That's hardly the way to win friends and have a happy life.

The roots of <u>all</u> those people go back far beyond memory, and probably beyond written record. Can't they honor their common heritage? There are edifices of many different cultures in Jerusalem. Each has meaning to its culture, but none of them denigrates other cultures. Their use by the local believers harms no one.

The turmoil in the Mideast is not really about religion. It is about exclusion. The west bank wall, like the Berlin wall, is not for safety, but for exclusion. Each wants to exclude the other. Exclusion will not make their lives better. If what your neighbors believe keeps them happy, that should help your faith keep you happy. What drives radical groups is not their neighbor's faith, but the fear of being excluded from their own. If we could eliminate the exclusivity of both sides, the problems would seem trivial. Settlements in the West Bank were not the problem. It was that they were exclusively Jewish.

In the process of evacuating Gaza, the Jews are destroying everything that was there. What purpose does that destruction serve? The real solution is to build, not to destroy. What's wrong with a Palestinian living in a house that was built by Jews on Palestinian territory 40 years ago? Don't tear down the settlements, just open them to Jews and Arabs alike. Don't dismantle the family businesses that have been the dedicated labor of preceding generations—open them to Jews and Palestinians alike. Don't throw the Jews out—join them! Driving them from their homes is the source of the hatred.

The Old Testament does indeed contain "An eye for and eye and a tooth for a tooth." (Exodus 24-26) But retribution and vengeance have never worked in the Mideast or anywhere else. Religious leaders on both sides have an enormous opportunity to change that course of history by preaching what they claim to be the tenets of their respective religions—love and cooperation. They haven't so far. Every religion wants to recruit new followers. Calling everyone else evil goes counter to that concept.

Today, clerics on both sides support the pursuit of dominance. Instead of rising above the conflict, they have entered it. That's not what their followers really want. They want peace and stability. Since religion is based on faith, the faithful follow their leaders even when they are off track. It is extremely unlikely that the people will rise against their own clerics and get them back on track. Those clerics should take a page from Pope Benedict's book. He was visiting synagogues and mosques and teaching tolerance and understanding. But no! They castigated him for saying, truthfully, that Islam had accepted violence in the past—as, in fact, had both the Jews and the Christians. People have far more in common than they do in conflict. Why must we focus on our differences rather than our similarities? The two sides have common goals, which they can reach if they do it together.

Perhaps this is symptomatic of man's struggle worldwide. In Germany the Arians wanted to exclude the Jews. In Rwanda the Tutsis want to exclude the Hutus. In Northern Ireland the Protestants want to exclude the Catholics. In Iraq, the Shiites want to exclude the Sunnis and Kurds as well as the Americans. But exclusion has never worked——inclusion has. Even in the United States we fight over exclusion despite the fact that we are the world's greatest example of the power of inclusion. Whites want to exclude blacks, Hispanics want to exclude Asians and straights want to exclude homosexuals. In no instance do these cultural differences cause the others harm. It is the effort to exclude that causes the conflict. Note that it was not the immigrants who came to America and collected in ghettos that built this country. It was their children who left the ghetto and used the diversity around them to build the greatest nation on earth.

Jesus of Nazareth, Mahatma Gandhi, Nelson Mandela, and Martin Luther King Jr. taught their followers to get along with the adversary instead of getting back at him. Their remarkable success makes one wonder why that goal is so elusive today. Why can't the rest of us hear their message? It works!

The United States is complicit in this unrest. Since Israel's formation in 1948, we have supported it financially and militarily, even when they were wrong and when they defied us. There is reasonable doubt that Israel would even exist today without that support. We have helped them become terrible neighbors. Here, then is our great opportunity. If we want to contribute to a peaceful Mideast, we must make it clear to Israel that we support them as long as they are good neighbors. We will support their inclusiveness, not their exclusiveness. And, in the interests of peace we will not support them militarily. To the extent that they abuse our support by seeking dominance at the expense of peace they will lose that support.

But the sword cuts both ways. Palestinians, who want more than their territory back and want to exclude the Jews, must also get that message. Hamas wants to destroy Israel. If they want our support, they too must earn it by being good neighbors. We are proud to call ourselves the melting pot. If we really believe in that, inclusiveness is what we should preach.

Many thousands of lives have been shed for that simple unspoken word "Exclusive." How many more must be shed before it is clear that vengeance, by its very nature, cannot succeed? Anyone who has ever weeded a garden knows that ethnic cleansing doesn't work. Vengeance merely brings more victims and more resolve into a conflict that cannot be won and should not be won. Imagine the progress a cooperative and peaceful society could make in the cradle of mankind—a barren place that, with Man's remarkable ingenuity, can be so bountiful that all who see it want to be there, but which for two hundred generations of man has failed to reach that potential. Let's give it a chance.

CHAPTER 33
The Devil's Workshop

Drug use in America today is frightening. Great numbers of people are addicted, injured or even killed by this epidemic.. It is perpetuated by money-grabbing drug lords who have only one interest—making money at what ever cost it takes. Make no mistake—they are good at what they do! They know who is vulnerable and how to reach them. Few people become addicted to drugs after they are 25 years old. Most of the damage begins in the early teens, and comes to fruition in the late teens and early twenties. Ask any addict when she started, and it is usually around age 13 to 15. (It's getting younger. Ten years ago it was 16, and tomorrow it may be 11). So that is the target market.

What can we do about it? Is it possible that these drug lords are merely preying upon a societal weakness we don't recognize? What do we expect of our teenagers? Are they occupied? Do they have goals? Do they have demands placed upon them? Society places demands upon everyone——except a teenager. Teenagers get a free ride until all of a sudden they meet demands and obligations when they get out of school and decide to raise a family. Most of them are unprepared for that change.

Idle hands are the devil's workshop. Today teenagers' hands are, for the most part, idle and the drug culture thrives in that workshop. Note also, that in most families today, both parents, or the only parent, work. They are not home to supervise. The hours between 3:00 PM when school lets out and 6:00 PM when a parent gets home are the drug dealer's gold mine.

Meanwhile the demand for an education is increasing every year. It is harder and harder to get job without an education unless you want to wash dishes in a restaurant for the rest of your life. We are facing declining education levels throughout our society. Can that explain why almost 30% of our college students are foreign born? (Almost 60% of our graduate students are foreign born.)

These problems are related. We don't challenge our teenagers enough. We don't educate them enough. Teenagers are extremely curious and have boundless energy. Perhaps we should extend the school day by an hour. Teachers will hate that. If we use that time to gain on our education gap we will compete with the drug dealers for the student's time. Cut out a third of the idle time available to the drug dealers. Give the students more, as well as more challenging assignments——ones that apply to the life they'll lead when they get out of school.

Life is about accomplishment. Man is the only creature who has developed the ability to improve our world. What has he done with that capacity? He has come close to destroying it. The abuse far exceeds the use and development. Aren't we adding to that disconnect by making life too easy for our teenagers? They have a right to accomplish too! Why not give them some help?

It would also be wise to increase our after school activities. Healthy productive ones like sports, music, art, public service, reading, hiking, studying the environment, studying global warming and its causes and cures. There is no shortage of tasks that teenagers, with their boundless energy, can accomplish. Give them a hand and let them get a feeling of accomplishment, instead of getting a fake one through drugs and getting high. The very best high is the high of getting something done you thought you couldn't do. Smoking weed can't compare with that, but we don't give them a chance to find that out for themselves.

Teenagers, like everyone else, want to feel good. Give them a chance to feel good about themselves as well. Provide a host of productive opportunities. Don't make them look for artificial highs that will sap their energy and creativity but accomplish nothing. Push them to achieve, because they'll never understand how it feels to accomplish a difficult task until they've done it. That's what we should do with an extra hour of school every day. Put teenagers idle time to productive use, and eventually, they'll love you for it.

Everyone wants their children to have a better life than they have. But we tend to equate better with easier. Easier is rarely better, and usually is far worse. Giving kids a free ride certainly doesn't help them, and it gives us a society of disabled people who need help instead of giving help. Is that the world you want for your kids?

Teachers may hate my idea, but what are they teachers for? Aren't they motivated to make the next generation the best generation ever? If not, why are they teachers? Perhaps they, too, have had an unproductive youth and don't know the feeling of accomplishment. Here's their chance to learn!

Public schools should close at 4:00 PM not 3:00 PM. Every student should have a yearlong after-school assignment they should accomplish either alone or in cooperation with other students, or even their parents. They should plan it, report on it and work on it at times when they feel they can best accomplish the task. That will require some critical thinking. They must present a schedule to the school. They should write a report on it at the end of the school year, beginning in third grade, and get graded on it.

Our students have more ability than we give them credit for. Just watch them on the computer or the cell phone. If we expect more from them we will not only get more from them we will prepare them for the competitive life they will face when they graduate and have to compete for a job against Chinese, Indian and Japanese students. Today they are at a distinct disadvantage. They don't learn how to apply themselves to challenging tasks. That is our fault, not theirs.

How would you challenge your kids? How will you give your kids a feeling of accomplishment rather, than a feeling of boredom?

CHAPTER 34
Bio-fuels—A Fad?

We do indeed face an energy shortage. Unfortunately, it is largely political right now, but long term it is real. Oil, our main energy source, is not only largely in the political control of unstable and unfriendly nations, its supply is grossly overstated. The problems with oil are threefold: First, is the whimsical supply in unstable or antagonistic governments; Second, it is a greenhouse gas emitter; Third, it is a depleting finite resource. We will run out! Bio fuels mitigate two of these problems, but not the third. They eliminate none of them.

Bio-fuels do reduce our demand for oil from antagonistic or greedy countries.

Bio-fuels produce as much or more greenhouse gases as fossil fuels. So, they are no help in global warming and climate change. That means that they are a temporary solution to part the problem.

We must be realistic about bio fuels. If we were to take our entire corn crop and convert it to fuel grade ethanol, it would barely supply 8% of our gasoline demand. Meanwhile what would we feed our cattle? Meat prices have already jumped over 50%. As we convert more acreage to corn from other products, such as wheat, the price of bread has risen 40%. There has to be a better way. There IS a better way!

I am not an enthusiast of bio-fuels but I do believe that they can serve a useful purpose in today's global world if we plan well and manage even better. We are doing neither today. Let's begin with a caveat—bio-fuels must not be derived from the conversion of other marketable products to bio-fuels. Don't rely on corn! It already has a purpose and a common usage. Don't mess! What about the corn stalks after the harvest? They can be converted to bio-fuels—they, too, are made of cellulose, which can be fermented like corn. They currently have no other usage. What about wheat chaff or straw? Sugarcane residue? Grass clippings? (Fill your gas tank at your local golf course.) We are not using our heads, let alone our resources.

Biofuels do have an advantage. We are in a recession and job losses are increasing. A new energy source will create new jobs to replace the ones we sent to China, India, Sumatra and Nigeria. Building another industry for bio-fuels would also help get the control of our energy resources out of the hands of those extremely profitable (and greedy) oil and coal companies. Got a better plan?

But let's not get carried away. There are serious weaknesses in a bio-fuel plan. Ethanol is made by fermentation—-a process that produces 95% as much CO2 as it does ethanol. Fermented ethanol, therefore, is far worse as a greenhouse gas emitter than gasoline. In addition, ethanol produces only 68% as much energy per pound as gasoline. Because of that it is a worse greenhouse gas emitter than gasoline even after it is made. How will that affect our global warming? That's why bio-fuels are a temporary solution. Still better, there are at least two commercial processes for making ethanol that do not produce equal amounts of carbon dioxide. Why not use them? We have to do better!

There are those who claim that biofuels are "carbon neutral." They claim that the corn used atmospheric carbon dioxide to grow, so we are merely returning that carbon dioxide to the atmosphere. Fossil fuels also grew out of atmospheric carbon dioxide that was stored it in them for a million years. Why is storing it only one year an improvement? "Carbon neutral" is a hoax!

The science is way ahead of the technology. We know the chemistry of converting cellulose to fermentable sugars, but we haven't developed the technology to capitalize on it. A few companies use enzymes to make ethanol from waste cellulose. They are small, but cost-competitive. Their expansion would not only create alternatives to a disappearing resource, they would also employ displaced workers whose jobs were sent overseas. If we are good at it, we might be able to export some of that technology and reduce our negative balance of trade. Even more, because it is worse environmentally than gasoline, it would stimulate people's thinking on the ways of the future. What other ways do we have of bringing energy back to the people? Want to try hydrogen-enriched fuels? Maybe <u>you</u> have a <u>better</u> idea!

CHAPTER 35
Voting

I am disturbed by the fact that in the 2008 presidential campaigns, particularly the democratic primaries, the factors that seemed to count the most were the ones that should count least. Race and gender dominate much of the voting, when neither of these had any serious bearing on the candidates ability to lead. This points out a flaw in our treatment of elections. For some reason, our nation believes that becoming 18 suddenly makes one an expert in voting. (We don't think a 16th birthday suddenly confers driving competence on our youth.) Our press coverage always mentions race and gender, but pretends that they are not major considerations. If not, why mention it? A two-year old can tell you which candidate is black, and which candidate is female. But a 2-year-old is not able to determine who is a better leader. I suspect most 18 year-olds can't either.

Why, since voting is an essential part of a democracy, do we leave it to chance? Shouldn't we teach classes on sensible voting in all our public schools? Our voter turnout is very low among voting democracies worldwide. Many people, particularly the young, feel that their vote won't count. It assuredly won't if they don't cast it!

How many new voters know that most elections are won by majorities of less than 55% of the votes cast? That means that, in an election involving 1000 voters, less than 100 votes usually determines the outcome. Actually, it is worse than that. In many elections, only 45% of eligible voters actually vote. That means that 46 electors decided the election, while 550 voters stayed home. This is democracy?

Democracy is participatory. If you don't participate, you will lose your democracy. That is happening in the United States. Political campaign expenditures have grown exponentially in the last three decades. But individual voters aren't spending that money——special interests are. A big corporation can't vote, but its Political Action Committee can buy lots of public advertising and television time. They will spend the money to glorify their point of view. Campaign financing is designed to persuade, not to inform. Does it seem responsible to you to spend $4 billion on a campaign to elect a person who gets paid $375,000 a year while 2 million children don't have enough to eat?

Voters should be taught about those manipulations and how to cut through them. Voters should not be asking what the candidate wishes will happen so much as how the candidate will achieve it. If you look at the utopian picture most candidates paint of the future they seek, you will find that they are remarkably similar. But look instead at what they will do to achieve that Promised Land. There you'll find differences. What have they done in the past to better the world they want to run? There, again, you will find wide differences. Don't press candidates for the failures of his opponents, but press them for their own successes. Oddly enough, the list of failures a candidate points out in an opponent is much longer than the list of his own successes. Therein lies the value of voter information. No one succeeds at everything they do. A candidate's successes are the clues to what that candidate will do if elected.

Voting should be a required course in every public school. It should be taught in ninth or tenth grade—before the legal age of quitting school. It should cover techniques for getting the real facts about the candidates and for cutting through the rhetoric to facts about what they have done and what they are planning to do. It should contain data on close elections and expose some of the evils of uninformed voting in the past.

Such a course might alleviate another problem—voter registration. When a student completes the course, they should be issued a voter certification card, that contains their date of birth. The card will act as their voter registration ID in any state in the future. This process will not eliminate the problem of voter registration, but it will greatly reduce it.

If we all learn a little about the receiving end of campaigning, we would have better elections and better elected representatives. We would not be focusing on race or gender, which basically aren't critical, but on issues that are! Will your schools teach your children to vote? They will if you make them!

CHAPTER 36
Reading—Our Lost Art?

I am appalled by the number of people who find reading a tiresome task instead of a source of joy. Reading is probably one of the oldest and most defining of human skills. It was reading that separated man from all other living creatures by giving us the ability to learn from someone we never even met. No other animal can do that. Reading, however, is no longer the only way by which we can learn from past or distant mentors. Movies, radio, television and now the Internet and cell phones—all provide means of vicarious learning.

There is one major difference between reading and most of those others. In reading, the choice is yours. Not so in movies, on television or on the radio, where the choice is made by someone who has an agenda of his own. "Can I make money on it?" The Internet differs from the other non-reading media, for. it allows you to make the choice. You get from the Internet what you want—-not just what some advertising mogul thinks he can make a buck on.

The Internet is a seminal change in society and we have not yet learned how to use it properly. Like most other new things, it is abused at least as much as it is used. I get two to three e-mails every week offering me pornographic literature and pictures. I don't want these, I didn't' t ask for them and I don't read them. But they keep coming. As fast as I get my name off one mailing list, some other porn pusher puts me on his—with no encouragement whatsoever. There isn't a "no call" list on the Internet, and the spam control we have doesn't work particularly well.

I am inclined to think that the Internet is a good thing but it presents endless opportunity for abuse, and it has markedly decreased the interest in reading. That is a serious loss. The computer age is founded on the idea that electronics can make things easier. It is easier to watch TV than to read——it is all done for you. All you have to do is open a beer and look. You don't even have to make it pass through your brain——just look.

I see this as symbolic of an age of vegetating. We are becoming a race of beings for whom things are done——not who do things. Skiing is replaced by snowmobiling. In the former you must learn the skill of skiing——in the latter you just push the starter and roar over your neighbor's raspberry bushes painting them with partially burned fuel. Motor boating has long since replaced sailing. Again you don't have to learn anything. Just push the starter and race over the nearest manatee leaving an oil slick on the kelp. Today's teenager can't walk. They have to drive or, more likely, be driven. Somehow, that time saved doesn't translate into productive time like reading to enrich the mind. They are too busy buying Pepsi and Tostados. They watch whatever the advertising moguls show him, rather than seek out their own course toward their own goals and their own desires. They accept the goals that TV presents and buy the products they push.

In our fast paced society I suspect that a course in speed-reading should be a required course in every middle school. Most people could read at two or three times the rate they now do and get more from the reading. They could more easily catch the flow and excitement of ideas in a more lifelike pace. But society is going the other way. We are not presenting reading as the joyful resource of independent ideas that it is. We aren't giving reading much more than lip service. It is a basic skill that is a requirement for a truly independent lifestyle. Escape the stereotype of the TV sitcom and find facets of life that never make it on TV. If we taught reading as the fine art that it is, and refined that skill at transferring information, we could open new vistas of ideas to our young as well as their parents. But our schools have adopted the insane idea that kids will learn to read by themselves—we don't really have to teach reading. It is too hard!

We have an immensely diverse world. Most of that diversity is lost on the bulk of our population. Could that be a part of the reason that we are destroying much of that diversity to make more condominiums and extract more commercial value out of nature's provisions? Is that why we see a forest as a source of lumber rather than an entire ecosystem that has secrets to tell us about every facet of life? Is that why the Alaskan Wildlife Refuge is seen as a source of an outmoded energy instead of world of different creatures from which we can learn?

I do not pass judgment on the Internet. It has the potential to benefit society, but also has the potential to damage it severely. There is no such thing as privacy on the Internet. Those who trust in "privacy policies" will soon find that they are a sham. You will be "cookied" to death by all the commercial interests that want their share of the profit available through the Internet. Reading allows you to escape all that. No one plants a cookie in your book. Budweiser doesn't know that you read "Silent Spring" and can't pressure you to buy an economy twelve pack because you did.

That world is being changed by advancing technology. In publishing, for example, a major change began more than 25 years ago when many publishers stopped accepting submissions by authors. Only agent's submissions were accepted. That shifted the burden of critical evaluation to the agents—one they accepted for less than ten years. That too, was slowly abandoned. Agents no longer make critical evaluations of submissions, nor do they market books. They read press releases about the author. They select the authors that sell well, but ignore those without previous commercial successes. Why do you suppose the author's name is larger than the title on about 75% of the books published today? Today, it is the author who markets a book. Agents and publishers merely capitalize on his work. The "great" authors of today are the ones who are also good marketers.

In recent years, newspapers began eliminating book reviews from their publications. Libraries have no readers who are willing to write reviews of new books by new authors. The sources of literary reviews are vanishing. The new author's challenge is to get anyone to read his book before they reject it. 90% of rejections are for books unread by the rejecter.

This is part of another major change. Companies hire survey teams to find out what the buying public wants. When they find out, they mass produce it and advertise it everywhere—and very creatively too! They make not the slightest effort to separate want from need. They sell chocolate cookies to five-year-olds because the survey shows that they want them. Let the dentists make money on the consequences. They don't want you to read, because they can't put an ad in your book! They want you to see it on television so they can push their fast foods. Then, when we get too fat on fast foods, they advertise myriads of "effortless" diet pills. They push cholesterol reducers and blood pressure depressants. They have millions of quick cures for the self-indulgence they promote with about 50 billion advertising dollars every year. And that, of course, is another source of profit.

It is time we looked at reading as the valuable resource of independence that it is. Instead of teaching the simple ABC's, we should teach the art of enjoying skillful, rapid and selective reading. In our information age, the problem is not getting information. The problem is finding what you need in the frivolous information overload that obscures it. Reading solves a great part of that problem. Let's learn it and learn it well. A nation of skillful readers will be a nation of independent thinkers who can learn to capitalize on diverse ideas from diverse cultures and from nature. Such readers will not be at the mercy of the ad man. They will not be assailed by the porn kings who can make a buck on those deprived individuals who can't make a healthy connection in life. Reading is indeed an ancient art but one that has yet to be developed into its true potential. It's time that the information age corrected that.

CHAPTER 37
Capital Gains—A Gift?

One of the big issues when budget time comes to Congress is the capital gains tax. That is a political issue, but it shouldn't be. Everyone is for capital gains tax relief, but how do we define capital gains? The original purpose of such tax relief was claimed to be the encouragement of investment in new companies, new equipment and new ideas to create new business, new jobs and new opportunities. Capital gains tax relief should do exactly that. The current system isn't even related to that concept. It is merely a gift to those wealthy enough to derive substantial income from longer-term investments. That's capital gains all right, but not for the intended purpose.

Buying stock in Exxon Mobil that you hold for a year is not investing capital in new ideas, jobs or opportunities. The company doesn't get any of that money—it goes to the former stockholder. Indeed, the company officers and directors, who hold large amounts of that stock, do get a tax relief when they sell a portion of their holdings, but not the corporation. Why not provide tax relief to investments that really do create new jobs, new companies, new technological advances, or new concepts? The fact that you hold a stock for a year has no bearing on what that money accomplishes.

I propose that investments in new companies or new partnerships, which actually receive your capital and make use of it to create something new or different be given tax relief. These are often high-risk investments, and deserve special consideration. If capital gains taxes were restricted solely to stocks bought directly from the company, not from another stockholder, they would serve the original purpose and the public as well. I propose that there be no tax on gains made on investments made in a company before it goes public, if you hold the stock for one year after it becomes publicly held. Tax only 20% of the gains if you sell the stock in its second year of being publicly held. Tax 40% of the tax gain if you sell the third year, 60% the fourth year or later, 80% in the fifth year. Thereafter the gain is taxed as income, which it is.

Such system would apply to anyone. Many small companies are started by middle or low-income people who have new ideas they can't accomplish through big corporations. If you redefine capital gains as those actually earned by investing in new ventures and new ideas, I strongly favor a capital gains tax reduction. But to offer tax relief merely because you have enough money to invest is counterproductive and will create no new jobs anywhere except at the IRS, or perhaps the capital investment firms.

CHAPTER 38
Profiling

We have a national debate over profiling as a security measure. The problem with the debate is that the definition of profiling is fuzzy at best and downright confusing often. There is a way to approach the problem sensibly.

The United States has been under terrorist attack for almost 30 years beginning with the internment of 400 American Embassy personnel in Iran in 1979. All those attacks were by Muslim extremists between 17 and 40 years old. This is fact, not conjecture. Conjecture is that Muslims are attacking the United States. Fact is that extremists are! Extremists are busy recruiting within the Muslim faith—Islam. This is not the first time extremists have tried to take over a religion. In the crusades in the 13th century, extremists tried to take over Christianity. It is a sad fact that religions tend to try to impose their beliefs on others. History shows that this is the rule, not the exception. Missionaries of many faiths exist throughout much of the world today. Most, but not all, are peaceful.

To ignore that fact is illogical. However, profiling need not be anathema. It need not be extreme. If we find an 18-year-old Arab at an airport gate, we should be alert, but we need not bother him. He merely requires a second look. We have merely identified a member of the terrorist's profile group. Terrorists have no rules against profiling. We don't know if he has in fact been targeted.

If the second look reveals that he is traveling on an expired visa, a falsified ID or with chemicals in his luggage, the look should be further intensified. The fact that he is a Muslim is not the reason for the detention. His own acts of suspicious nature are. We can subject him to successive levels of scrutiny, and release him if they come up negative. At each successive indication of terrorist connections, the level of scrutiny and of detention increases.

People are people. Each of us has some individual characteristics. When they present a threat to others there may be concern. If not, there should be none. Profiling can be a factor in protecting us from terrorism, but it need not be a punitive one. To ignore known risks is self-defeating.

CHAPTER 39
Gay Marriage

We have much public debate and furor over gay marriage. There should be none. Sexual activity is a private matter, and should remain so. It won't. We have a world full of people who think that they know how others should behave. Unless it impacts other lives private affairs should remain private. We would all be better off if they did.

Marriage is not a private matter only. It has at least two aspects that reach far beyond the two people involved. Marriage is confirmed by legal matters that involve inheritance, taxes and ownership rights. These aspects of marriage are in the control of governments—both local and national. There are other aspects of marriage, involving ethics, religious beliefs and the upbringing of children. These are not in the control of the State. Churches and religious organizations strongly influence these aspects of marriage as is testified by the fact that most marriages are performed in churches or at least by a cleric. The church has been increasingly involved in marriage for about 2500 years. However, the state was involved before that for the wealthy who wanted to make a public record of the legal aspects of marriage, primarily inheritance, property and ownership rights.

It is important to note that the two aspects of marriage, the state sponsored legal rights and the religious ethical issues are not the same. Neither holds sway over the other. Here is where the problems get intense. Marriage is first and foremost a commitment. Two people are committed to sharing their lives—every aspect of their lives. Basically that is what marriage is all about. During the twentieth century in this country, and in much of the rest if the world as well, that commitment has been weakening. Today almost 50% of marriages end up in divorce. That speaks volumes about the "commitment" part of marriage—its fundamental precept.

It turns out that nature, like all the rest of the universe, can make mistakes. One of the fundamental reasons for marriage is to assure that children will be cared for by parents who accept the obligation to raise them. Another reason for marriage was to assure that fathers could be identified in a society where men were completely dominant and women were subordinated. You can always tell who the mother is, but not the father. Marriage was an attempt to resolve that problem. Sex and reproduction do not require marriage. The shared care and tending as well as the inheritance of the offspring does. Human children cannot raise themselves. They are dependent upon others for five or more years of their lives—like it or not. As the level of sophistication of society grows, that demand becomes ever greater. Today, an education is an absolute requirement for a productive life no matter what you do in life. Most of that responsibility falls upon parents and the schools which society has established to fill that need. Two hundred years ago, a sixth grade education (the three R's) was adequate for most people. Today, a high school education is not adequate for a truly productive life.

There are other changes in society. Among them is the recognition that not everyone is heterosexual. There are people who are attracted to others of their same sex. This appears to be a native problem—you are born with it. In the past, this was a self-limiting problem. People who have sex with others of their own sex can't produce children. In that respect, they are not producing more genetic homosexuals. No one really knows what causes homosexuality, but certainly heredity could be a substantial factor. Is some of it learned or taught? We don't know. At least it is not deliberately taught.

Many believe that homosexuality is a personal choice. In our present society, which stigmatizes homosexuality, no one in their right mind would choose that lifestyle and the isolation and distrust it brings. Besides, for those who believe that, ask yourself this question—could you consciously change your sexual response from one of the opposite sex to one of your own?

Now here is where the problem becomes extremely complex. If two adults decide to commit to each other they have the right to do so. No one is hurt. In the case of a man and a woman, they sanctify that with a marriage ceremony. That satisfies both the legal and the religious aspects of the commitment. They achieve the legal and the religious valediction of their commitment, and also acquire some obligations—both legal and religious.

Suppose we have a same sex couple what are willing to make that same commitment. They face a problem. Most religions define marriage as a union between a man and a woman. The legal aspects of marriage—the legal status, the inheritance, the property rights and other legal rights—are conferred by the state, local or national government—not by the religion.

Where is the dilemma? Howard Dean had it right. The state can confer the legal and property rights of the union, but has no authority to provide the religious rights of marriage. Why call it marriage? That only serves is to antagonize the religious community. Civil Union is exactly that. It legally confers those aspects of marriage that are within the control of the state to a committed couple. The religious aspects of "Marriage" are reserved for the religion involved. Religions need not sanctify it, but they will not eliminate the legal rights of a committed union.

In a world that takes such a dim view of "Commitment" that half of marriages end up in divorce, who can deny two same sex people the legal right to make that commitment? By the same token, why antagonize half the world by calling it "marriage", a term that for six millennia has meant a union of two people of opposite sex for the purpose of having a family? Who is helped by such terminology? It can't help the legal aspects of the union, and it can't even address its religious aspects. Do you really believe that sanctifying the name "marriage" by the state will convince the religious opponents? Not a chance.

That brings us to other aspects of same-sex unions in our technically advanced society—children. Same sex couples cannot have children. But they can adopt them or have surrogate parents, or have biological implants of viable embryos. Many people oppose such practices, but there is no evidence that they can't be good parents. No one knows if they will purposely or accidentally teach their children to be homosexual. And assuredly many traditional marriages already fail in the upbringing of their children. Do we have any evidence that homosexual unions are necessarily bad parents, or produce homosexual children? None that I've ever heard of. So far all homosexuals came from heterosexual families, so there is nothing to say that limiting parenting to heterosexual families will curtail or eliminate homosexuals in the future.

Because of divorce, we already have many single parent families. Are they necessarily worse parents? Worse than two parents of the same sex? Just for tranquility it might be desirable to have fewer, or no homosexuals in the future, but tranquility is not sufficient reason to manage society. We haven't eliminated homosexuality in 6,000 years so far. There is no reason to believe that we would be better off if we had. Some homosexuals, like Socrates and Tchaikovsky and Oscar Wilde, have been remarkably productive. We still have a lot to learn! Let's not make the changing of a six thousand year old word a battleground which only tries to have one side try to prove the other side wrong.

CHAPTER 40
Unintended Consequences

Our world becomes more complex every day, so it is ever more difficult to fathom the full range of consequences, ideas and actions that we produce. Some of the most successful creations of man have had nearly devastating consequences, many of which could not have been foreseen. DDT, and Fluorocarbon technology are good examples of such unanticipated problems that resulted because the products were far better than originally thought. Probably the most far-reaching new creation is the remarkable advance in medical technology. It has saved untold numbers of lives and relieved unfathomable quantities of suffering. Even this marvelous result is not without its downside. In medicine, the downside is still approaching, but rapidly and almost unnoticed.

Modern medicine is really just over 100 years old. Aspirin was a precursor of this revolution in medical technology. Invented in 1894 aspirin first became widespread in WWI. It was one of the first man-made medicines. Prior to that most medicines were derived from natural products. Herbs and extracts of natural products were essentially the only sources of medical treatment until aspirin. Even today, a substantial proportion of new medicines have herbal or natural origins. Taxol, for instance was not invented for treatment of cancer, but discovered.

Aspirin was only the precursor. It demonstrated that man could make products that were beneficial to health. And the search began. Some early successes were penicillin and streptomycin. Invented in the 1930's, they were slow to find public usage. Actually penicillin was invented before the mycin drugs, but was not developed until a little later. WWII was the big booster of Penicillin and brought it to the market. At first it was only available to our military until the production capabilities were ramped up considerably. Then it became so universal that, as is often the case, it was overused in places it was unneeded, and produced several strains of drug resistant microbes. We are facing those today.

The big unintended consequence of medical advances is just coming to fruition. Population explosion. Modern medicine has so greatly reduced infant mortality that the population of our world has suddenly exploded. The world's population was increasing at about 1/2% per year up until about 1900. Since then it has exploded, and currently is growing at almost 3% per year. That may not seem like a bad thing, but carried to the extreme toward which we are headed, it poses an immense problem.

The world is finite. It can't grow. But mankind is becoming infinite. Malthus was right. He said since our food resources grow at an arithmetic pace, but our population grows exponentially, it is absolutely inevitable that we will outgrow our food supply at some time. Technology and advanced farming techniques may slow down the problem, but they can't eliminate it. So the problem grows worse as we take ever more agricultural land and convert it to housing developments. We add to the population while reducing our sources of food for that population. Today 1.2 billion people, almost 20% of our world's population, live in extreme poverty. Eleven million children under five die each year from starvation and malnutrition-induced illnesses. Starvation and malnutrition are the largest causes of death worldwide, and rising. If we keep on growing our population the way we are today, our children or our grandchildren will be faced with the unholy task of deciding which of their fellow humans shall live and which shall die. That is a circumstance to be avoided at all costs. Is that the world those dedicated pioneering medical inventors sought?

Nature is bountiful. Essentially all viable species produce far more offspring than are required to sustain their population. Great numbers of them die or are eaten or starved long before they reach maturity. Such was the case of early man—until medicine changed the dynamic. We suddenly decreased the percentage of infants that failed to reach maturity but we didn't limit the production of infants. These are somewhat self-limiting. In 1865, the average U.S. family had about six children. Rarely did all of them reach maturity. In fact, on average less than 2/3 of them did. Infant mortality was high and childbed fever took many young mothers. Nevertheless, we had a rapidly expanding population even then. We also had more than 2/3 of our nation undeveloped and essentially unpopulated. In that agricultural society, children were an economic asset. They began working on the farm as early as 4 years old. They had chores and duties around the house and yard that supplemented the family resources. They soon matured and allowed the family to expand their farms into unoccupied territory.

With the industrial revolution, families were moving out of farms and into cities. Children suddenly became a financial burden rather than an asset. Children can't help you if you work in a factory. So family size began to shrink. This was a gradual transition.

In other nations, the availability of medicines from foreign countries was rapid and unbalanced. Family size is still eight in most Arab countries and their populations are exploding. In fact, they are proud of that fact and claim that they will take over the world merely by out producing offspring. The average age in Iraq is 19. That, unfortunately, fails to recognize one point. The areas into which they can expand are already occupied, and will be fought over bitterly and forcefully. That is happening in the Mideast right now! That entire area is besieged by battles among ethnic groups over diminishing resources.

The unintended consequence of such a benevolent event as advanced medical technology did not foresee that a necessary companion to that development was the limiting of family size. It may be a disturbing point that when we produced medical life-saving technology, we were changing the balance of nature. We need to compensate with other advances—such as birth control. This is an effort that must be done consciously today, if we are to avoid its being forced upon us in the near future. It is the desire of families not just to have children, but to produce succeeding generations of adults. So, as we increase the percentage that reach adulthood we must decrease numbers we produce. That, sadly, is one of the untaught lessons of advanced medical science. As we fail to teach that today, it will be forced upon our grandchildren painfully and forcefully. They will face a world where population is limited by survival. The majority of people will be miserable in a subsistence economy. Since almost 1/4 of the world is in such a state today, do we doubt that it will happen? The reproductive dynamic of today is inevitably forcing us into a world where starvation will be the factor controlling world population. Bitter battles will be fought over territory and ownership. In the Mideast today, the Shiites and the Sunni's are fighting among themselves even more than they are fighting the infidels. Is this a precursor to future world politics?

There are about 6.4 billion people on earth today. At our current growth rate there will be 12 billion by 2040. But we don't yet know if this earth is large and fertile enough to sustain the 6 billion already here. And by 2075 the projections are that we will have 24 billion. Think of a world where you see four people everywhere you see one today.

There is an additional error in our modern medical approach. Most of our medical advances are designed to manage or control the myriad ailments to which we are subject. That leaves us with a world of ailing people controlling their ailments and producing children subject to similar ailments. We may think that the survival of the fittest is too harsh to apply to human beings, but that is how we got here. It applies whether we like it or not. To capitalize on that, most of our medical research should be focused on prevention or cure——not on maintenance and control. Until about 1700, most hemophiliacs died before they reached maturity. Today they live and produce more hemophiliacs. Do I oppose hemophiliacs? Not at all, but I feel we short-change them. What we want to do is cure them, not maintain them. Our studies in genetics already allow us to alter our DNA. I'm not sure that is a good idea, but it certainly would help hemophiliacs. We have in our possession a powerful tool—-let's look for the unintended consequences before we distribute it broadly. What can we learn from DDT that, among other things, made the native peregrine falcon extinct east of the Mississippi?

Of course we should keep inventing medicines and treatments, but we must be much more thoughtful long term on how we do so. Governments should not support research on maintenance and control, but only on cure and prevention. If we are to use DNA studies for health, make sure it is to produce a less susceptible mankind, not a more susceptible one. Let's make sure medical research is to make mankind better, not to make drug companies rich.